HOOKED RUG PORTRAITS

ANNE-MARIE LITTENBERG

Published by
STACKPOLE BOOKS
5067 Ritter Road
Mechanicsburg, PA 17055
www.stackpolebooks.com

Customer Service (877) 462-2604
www.rughookingmagazine.com

On the front cover: *Esther*, designed and hooked by Patty Yoder.
On the back cover: *Leo*, designed and hooked by Diane Phillips.
Photographs by Anne-Marie Littenberg unless otherwise noted.

Library of Congress Cataloging-in-Publication Data

Littenberg, Anne-Marie.
Hooked rug portraits/ Anne-Marie Littenberg.—1st ed. p. cm.
Includes bibliographical references and index.
   ISBN 978-1-881982-73-9
    1. Rugs, Hooked—Patterns. 2. Portrait drawing. I. Title.
   TT850.L58 2011
   746.7'4—dc22
                2010050643

CONTENTS

DEDICATION

This book is dedicated with love in memory of my Dearest Poppy. Your children, grandchildren, and great-grandchildren miss you but are so grateful for all the time we had together, and the joy you brought to Our Most Wonderful Mom.

ACKNOWLEDGMENTS

I want to acknowledge the women in my two rug hooking groups: The Nine and Friday Hooking. You have taught me so much about color, design, technique, and critique. You have shared your wool and hooks and frames . . . and snacks. Yes, there must always be snacks! You have loved me and provided life-saving care and nurturing during very dark times. Together we have laughed, cried, yelled, and loved. You are always in my heart. You are (in alphabetical order) Polly Alexander, Kathy Borie, Eugenie Delaney, Suzanne Dirmaier, Molly Dye, Cindy Godin, Rae Harrell, Barbara Held, Diane Kelly, Jen Lavoie, Lynn Ocone, Celia Oliver, Diane Phillips, Jule Marie Smith, and the late Patty Yoder.

CHAPTER 1

What Is a Hooked Rug Portrait?

Europa, 39" x 37", hand-cut, hand-dyed wool on rug warp. Designed and hooked by Jule Marie Smith, Ballston Spa, New York, 1989.

A figure from Greek mythology, Europa is bordered by swirling clouds above and undersea life below.

Paintings and photographs may spring to mind when you think of portraits, but portraits have been created from myriad materials for as long as anyone has had the idea of making a representation of a person or animal.

Portraits have been in existence for thousands of years. In 1323 BCE, Tutankhamen's portrait was carved, painted, and gilded on his wooden sarcophagus. Ancient Romans depicted

their Caesars on coins. Alexander the Great's beloved horse, Bucephalus (who died in 326 BCE), was memorialized in a sculpture of precious metal. Itinerant painters created portraits of early American settlers throughout the colonies. Abraham Lincoln is glorified in marble on The Mall in Washington, D.C.

Rug hooking, though relatively new in terms of the history of art and craft, is a wonderfully creative medium for portraits. And in recent years, hooked rugs—whether as bed, floor, or wall coverings—have become a popular medium for rug hookers to render artistic depictions of people and pets.

Why create a hooked rug portrait? A portrait in wool allows us rug hookers to communicate feelings about a subject without using words. We can add personal elements to the composition to give the image special

Remembering, 14" x 14", #6- to 8-cut hand-dyed, over-dyed, and as-is wool on linen. Designed and hooked by Diane Phillips, Fairport, New York, 2004.

Aunt Eunice Comes Home, 42" x 36", #3- and 4-cut hand-dyed and as-is wool on monk's cloth. Designed and hooked by Suzanne Dirmaier, Waterbury Center, Vermont, 1995.

"This rug was inspired by a photograph taken of my great-great-great-aunt Eunice, my great-grandfather G.W. Rogers, his wife Ruth, and the dog Fido in front of the family homestead in Newport Center, Vermont. Eunice was a fire-and-brimstone Northern Baptist who outlived her siblings and children. In later years, my great-aunt Mabel had a charcoal sketch made from the photo but purposely omitted Eunice, who had told her too often to 'be seen and not heard.' Years later, my mother gave me the original photograph and corresponding charcoal sketch. The names hooked in the border are copied from family autograph albums to recreate the subjects' original signatures."

meaning. We may want to celebrate the accomplishments of a famous person, express our feelings for a beloved pet, or honor our family history. We may want to capture our own vision of characters from mythology or fiction.

Memories and old family photos are a constant source for portrait inspiration. Suzanne Dirmaier of Waterbury Center, Vermont, says, "Many of my rugs are meant to tell a story, and those are the ones that I like the best. I have a strong oral tradition in my family as my parents told me stories they heard from their parents. Rug hooking has given me a medium for cataloging some of those stories. I have come to know my family in a much deeper way. After I hooked *Aunt Eunice Comes Home,* I felt as if I knew her even though she died long before I was born."

Lance, 16" x 22", #3- and 6-cut hand-dyed wool on linen. Designed and hooked by Laura Pierce, Petaluma, California, 2005. PHOTO COURTESY OF LAURA PIERCE

In 2005, the American Folk Art Museum challenged rug hookers to create images representing icons of America. Laura was inspired by Lance Armstrong, seven-time winner of the Tour de France, cancer survivor, and founder of the Lance Armstrong Foundation. She included a bald eagle to emphasize his role on the American team. Yellow dots signifying the color that's been associated with the athlete race around the border.

As you start to plan your hooked rug portrait, consider what style most appeals to you.

- Do you want to create a representation that is precisely faithful in appearance?
- Do you want to create an idealization emphasizing particularly admired qualities?

Historically, portraits focused on creating images that were precise representations, cataloging how someone looked for posterity. Throughout most of human history, portraits were made only of royalty and important leaders in government, warfare, and business. Since the 19th century, portraits of everyday people at everyday tasks have risen in popularity.

Today, everyone has cameras, and photographic portraiture has freed artists from the obligation to create precise imitations of nature. You can flatter or acknowledge the uniqueness of your subject. You can pursue the inner essence of your loved one and keep memory alive, tell a story, express your feelings, or honor your subject. Most importantly, you can take pleasure in translating your vision into a hooked rug portrait.

The More Things Change, the More They Stay the Same, 19" x 13", #4-cut hand-dyed and as-is wool on linen. Designed and hooked by Suzanne Dirmaier, Waterbury Center, Vermont, 2009.

Mallets Bay on Lake Champlain, Vermont, is home to a summer cabin that has been owned continuously by the same family since 1907. The current occupants enjoy many of the same rituals of their forebears, including gathering on the porch for cocktails during warm summer evenings. This rug was inspired by an old photo of such a gathering from an earlier time. Suzanne did not copy the photo. Rather, she adapted the elements she found most interesting and appropriate to her composition. She eliminated figures from the original photo and changed the background to make it more pleasing. In addition, she designed one of the figures to resemble the current mistress of the cabin. While drawn to the ideas embodied by the original photo, Suzanne was not hampered by reality. She used her artistic vision to redesign the composition to adhere to her own vision.

Under September Sky, 37" x 32", hand-cut, hand-dyed, and as-is wool on linen. Designed and hooked by Rachelle LeBlanc, St. Albert, Alberta, Canada, 2010. PHOTO COURTESY OF RACHELLE LEBLANC

Rachelle believes in capturing those moments in life "that remind us we should all take time to see the beauty that surrounds us." Interest is added to the composition by having one foot rest on the edge while another steps outside the border.

Fatherhood: Papa, 24" x 25", hand-cut and hand-dyed wool and cashmere on linen. Designed and hooked by Rachelle LeBlanc, Montreal, Quebec, Canada, 2007.

PHOTO COURTESY OF RACHELLE LEBLANC

This rug is the first in a series titled "Fleeting Moments." According to Rachelle, "The series explores the passing moments that remind us of something precious, something that is hard to identify and thought forgotten." This rug was inspired by a photo taken of Rachelle's husband and newborn daughter. "She had been crying all day and the minute he took her in his arms, she fell asleep."

Pimento, 22" x 31", #6- to 8-cut hand-dyed, over-dyed, and as-is wool on linen. Designed and hooked by Diane Phillips, Fairport, New York, 2006.

Pimento was a much-loved companion of Diane's for many years. Diane believes that "by creating rugs that mirror what is going on in our minds and our lives, we come up with subject matter that makes the difference between what is interesting and boring." Anyone who has ever loved or been loved by a pet relates to the expression captured here in Pimento's eyes. The emotion evoked is realistic, even though fantasy colors are used in Pimento's coat and the size of his eyes has been greatly exaggerated and idealized.

Archie, 27" x 40", #6- to 8-cut hand-dyed, over-dyed, and as-is wool on linen. Designed and hooked by Diane Phillips, Fairport, New York, 2006.

Archie was one of Diane's beloved Bernese mountain dogs. She portrayed him with the fur color patterns classic to the breed. The image represents Archie's uniqueness by showing the dark birthmark spot on his snout, just between his eyes, and the different color patterns on his two front paws. As regal as his bearing may be, the back leg splays out at a realistic, comfortable angle.

Self Portrait, 15" x 15", plied threads of silk, wool, cotton, rayon, polyester, etc., on woven cotton. Designed and hooked by Anne-Marie Littenberg, Burlington, Vermont, 2005.

I am intrigued by self-portraits that show the artist in multiple views. To design this piece, I photographed myself looking into a mirror. I positioned the camera so it captured both my profile and the mirror's reflection. Note my right shoulder is kind of hunched up in both the reflection and profile views. This is because I was holding the camera up in my right hand when I snapped the image. When the portrait was completed, I was struck by how my profile was age-appropriate, but the reflection in the mirror showed me decades younger. This effect was not a conscious design choice, although I did make a point of showing the curl that is always sticking out on the back of my head.

Pandora, 31¹/₂" x 55", hand-cut, hand-dyed wool on rug warp. Designed and hooked by Jule Marie Smith, Ballston Spa, New York, 1988.

Jule was inspired by a character from Greek mythology. The composition is enhanced by the inclusion of elements from the story, including Pandora's Box.

Waiting for the Parade, 43" x 32", hand-cut and hand-dyed wool and cashmere on linen. Designed and hooked by Rachelle LeBlanc, Montreal, Quebec, Canada, 2007. PHOTO COURTESY OF RACHELLE LEBLANC

The composition of this rug was inspired by a black-and-white photo of Rachelle's Acadian grandmother (shown here in pink) as she waited for a victory celebration parade after World War II.

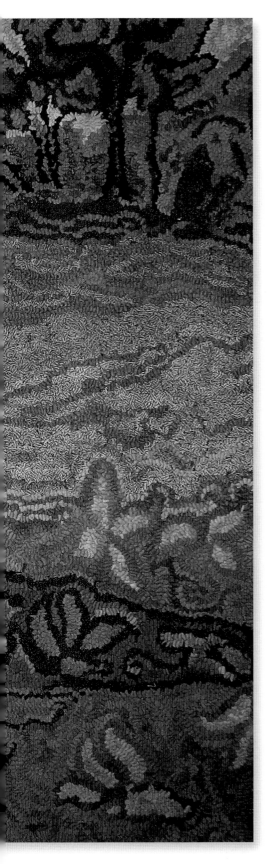

The Ann and Peg Show, 21½" x 19½", #3-cut hand-dyed wool, chenille yarn, and appliqué on cotton foundation. Designed and hooked by Peg Irish, Madbury, New Hampshire, 1998.

Peg was inspired by a photo of her with her good friend, Ann Winterling. She designed this piece by taking multiple photos of Ann seated and hooking. She based the couch on a public-domain clip art image. She says, "I tried to find the essence of us without hooking too much detail." Peg made print copies of rugs in progress and appliquéd them rather than trying to depict them with her hooking. She hooked the arms separately, and applied them later to achieve a three-dimensional effect. The miniature hooks were made from beads and wire. The floor is hooked on the reverse side of the backing. The back wall is a piece of dyed wool that was appliquéd around the figures.

CHAPTER 2

Studying Faces

Take some time to study faces in general as you begin to plan your hooked rug portrait. The easiest face to study is your own. Look at photographs of yourself posing from different angles and with various expressions: smiling, frowning, in profile, looking straight at the camera. What happens to the shape of your eyes when you smile compared to when you look solemn? Which features are most prominent when you look directly at the camera? Which are most prominent in profile? When I see my image in profile, I notice my strong nose. A

Dreaming of Blue Skies, 15" x 15½", #6- to 8-cut hand-dyed, over-dyed, and as-is wool on linen. Designed and hooked by Diane Phillips, Fairport, New York, 2007.

Diane includes garments in her portraits as a way to balance color. She says, "I usually don't have much garment showing, putting more emphasis and color in the hair and face. Sometimes, you cannot see any garments." Here, in addition to framing the face, the garment adds to the unspoken story.

14

Vincent van Gogh, 13½" x 15", #6- to 8-cut wool on monk's cloth. Designed and hooked by Gloria Reynolds Stokes, Hinesburg, Vermont, 2007.

This image of van Gogh fills the frame; it is an extreme close-up, so parts of his head are not in view. This perspective adds intensity to the piece. Filling the frame is a popular portrait technique in photography, and it adapts equally well to rug hooking.

photo of me looking straight at the camera emphasizes the height of my forehead.

Your face is more than just the outward appearance. Use your hands to feel the underlying bone and muscle structure. Compare how you look when peering in a mirror versus how you look in a photograph. Try to be objective. Subjective observations, such as "I hate my nose" or "I don't look as pretty as Vivien Leigh" are judgmental and will not help you in your efforts to learn how to draw the human face. Objective observations might be, "I have my grandmother's cheekbones" or "My sisters and I have the same color eyes." How do the muscles of your face change your looks when you try different facial expressions? I believe I look younger when I smile, and frowning, or an irritated expression, add a decade or two.

Compare the way the same face is shown in a painted portrait versus a photograph. Use a search engine on the Internet to look up both photos and paintings of the same person. What does Vincent van Gogh

Noah, 12" x 12", #6- to 8-cut hand-dyed, over-dyed, and as-is wool on linen. Designed and hooked by Diane Phillips, Fairport, New York, 2004.

"I hooked *Noah* while on vacation. I had only a limited amount of wool and had to use just what I had at hand. Blue wool used under his eye also appears in his hair, beard, and hand, and yet you have no trouble distinguishing the different features." According to Diane, "The old saying that color gets all the credit but value does all the work is true."

Suspicion, 10" x 11", #6- to 8-cut hand-dyed, over-dyed, and as-is wool on linen. Designed and hooked by Diane Phillips, Fairport, New York, 2004.

For Diane, faces evoke an emotional response. She never worries about making any of her faces glamorous. "I don't find glamour interesting. If you hook a face where it looks as though the person appears to be wearing lipstick and eye makeup, it tells you about the personality of the rug hooker and not about the portrayal on the backing. I would rather have character than glamour. If an image is striking, you think there is a story behind the face. When I design a rug, I imagine a story. If I am looking at a pretty image with makeup, it makes me think of a lipstick ad."

(1853–1890) look like in an old daguerreotype compared with one of his painted self-portraits? What about President Obama? How do ubiquitous images of him on T-shirts differ from his face on the evening news? How do the images differ in terms of the shapes and the proportion of the head, nose, and chin? What colors were used to depict hair and skin?

Keep a face journal. Go to a public place and try to sketch the faces you see. Do not worry about whether or not you "can" or "cannot" sketch. This exercise is purely for self-study; no one will judge your results. The purpose here is not to learn how to draw accurate representations. Rather, it is to help you observe the different shapes, colors, and expressions of people. What marks do you place in your sketch to indicate that someone is happy (a smile), worried (furrowed brow), or tired? Look through magazines and newspapers, or your own photo collection, and make a collage of the faces you find striking. Perhaps you choose a face because you love the subject (a family member), are attracted by

good looks (a movie star), or are moved by expressed emotions (from the newspaper).

Visit the portrait gallery of an art museum. If you cannot do this in person, then get on the Internet and explore portraits. Visit your local library and skim through books in the art collection. What colors did van Gogh use in his faces? How did the source of light in Rembrandt's (1606–1669) portraits affect shadows on faces? How did Matisse's (1869–1954) backgrounds compliment his portraits? Whose paintings depict faces of people who seem intensely real and human, even if the image is not like a photograph? (Alice Neel [1900–1984] is an excellent example.) Whose portraits were beautiful, idealized likenesses of his subjects? (Look up John Singer Sargent [1856–1925].) Who created powerful and often disturbing images that aren't portraits in the traditional sense but still have enormous emotional impact? (See any of Picasso's [1881–1973] works.) Who combined photography and paint in creating

Obama, 10" x 11", #6- to 8-cut hand-dyed, over-dyed, and as-is wool on linen. Designed and hooked by Diane Phillips, Fairport, New York, 2009.

Diane Phillips has hooked more than 40 faces. A few were inspired by photographs, but most come from her imagination. "When I sit down to do a face, I ask myself, do I want this person happy, thoughtful, inscrutable, or fierce?" According to Diane, the most important way of capturing someone's essence is through the eyes and the placement of the glint. Combine that with the centerline of the lip, and you have the person's mood. Do not worry about color planning.

contemporary portraits of the rich and famous? (Andy Warhol [1928–1987] made this technique his signature style.) Who photographs herself in the creation of portraits of imaginary people? (Look up Cindy Sherman [born 1954].)

By studying the faces of people in crowds, in paintings, in museums, and in images on the Internet, you learn about your own perceptions and how they compare and contrast with other artists in other media. Even if you don't consider yourself an artist, these exercises help to hone your rug hooking skills by suggesting new ideas for the use of color and for the design of your composition.

The Almost Virgin Queen (face detail) by Pat Merikallio. PHOTO COURTESY OF PHYLLIS FORD
A single color or value can be used for many applications throughout the hooked rug portrait. For example, the light blue under the eyes and along the nose of the Queen can also be found in her hair and throughout her ornate collar. (See the full rug on page 74.)

TIPS ON THE LAYOUT AND PROPORTION OF FACES

Leonardo da Vinci (1452–1519) believed it was important to understand proportion in humans and animals in order to accurately represent them in paint. While our medium is rug hooking and not paint, some of his basic concepts about proportion in human faces and heads are helpful to keep in mind. Grab a mirror and see if da Vinci's rules of proportion apply to your face.

- We often think of eyes as being located at the top of the face. However, they are actually located halfway between the very top of the head and the bottom point of the chin.
- The width of a face measures approximately five times the width of an eye.
- Eyes come in many shapes. However, the iris (the colored part of the eye) is always round. Part of it is usually hidden by either the upper or lower eyelid. The pupil is also round and always located in the center of the iris.
- The distance between the mouth and the bottom of the chin equals the width of the mouth.
- The distance between the base of the nose and the bottom of the chin is the same as the length of the nose. It is also the same as the length of the forehead.
- Eyebrows begin at the top of the nose. The distance from where the eyebrows begin to the bottom of the chin equals $2/3$ of the face.
- The space between the mouth and the bottom of the chin is the same as the tip of the chin to the throat.
- When looking straight ahead, the pupils line up with the outer corners of the mouth.
- The inner corners of the eyes line up with the widest points of the nose.
- The bottom of the earlobes line up with the bottom of the nose.
- The tops of ears line up with the tops of the eyes.

You can apply these points to any face you design. Of course, exceptions exist to every "rule," but these proportional guidelines provide a good approximation of the layout of most people's faces. Keep them in mind, but do not be a slave to them. In fact, if your creative juices are encouraging you to just design something spontaneously, go for it!

Mrs. Thomas, 15" x 19", #6- to 8-cut hand-dyed, over-dyed, and as-is wool on linen. Designed and hooked by Diane Phillips, Fairport, New York, 2006.

Mrs. Thomas was inspired by a photo Diane took of her neighbor. "I had a real willing model who let me take 20 photos of her and then pick the one I wanted to interpret. This rug looks like Mrs. Thomas, but it is an interpretation, not a copy of the photo. Obviously, she does not have multicolored braids or green and purple features."

Steve Fish (face detail) by Patty Yoder. (See the full rug on page 53.) Two simple lines of black, highlighted by a glint of white, depict deeply expressive eyes.

Color Play III, 10" x 12", #6- to 8-cut hand-dyed, over-dyed, and as-is wool on linen. Designed and hooked by Diane Phillips, Fairport, New York, 2007.

For Diane, part of the fun of hooking faces is that she does not have a lot of advance expectation about what the completed piece will look like. She lets it look like whatever it turns out to be. This approach is vastly different from trying to perfectly copy a photograph. "Starting with a photo isn't bad as long as you are willing to then go with whatever happens while you are hooking. Students are sometimes challenged by trying to translate a photo of a well-loved family member into an exact replica in wool. There can be a lot of emotional weight and investment in hooking a face from a photo." Diane suggests that one's first portrait project not involve copying a photograph with a lot of emotional significance. "Start with something that allows you the freedom to play and have fun."

Family Friends, 9¹/₂" x 10¹/₂", #6- to 8-cut hand-dyed, over-dyed, and as-is wool on linen. Designed and hooked by Diane Phillips, Fairport, New York, 2009.

Color Play I, 10" x 11", #6- to 8-cut hand-dyed, over-dyed, and as-is wool on linen. Designed and hooked by Diane Phillips, Fairport, New York, 2007.

Diane does little advance color planning or dyeing for her portraits. "Often, my backgrounds are based on what wool I have within reach of my chair." Diane suggests an exercise to experiment with value: Choose 10 pieces of wool that vary in value, then hook a portrait using only those 10 pieces.

Untitled 3, 15" x 15¹/₂", #6- to 8-cut hand-dyed, over-dyed, and as-is wool on linen. Designed and hooked by Diane Phillips, Fairport, New York, 2007.

When Diane begins hooking a face, the individual features can seem enormously exaggerated. "Eyes and noses initially look twice as large as they will when the piece is finished. Be patient. Resist the urge to tear them out and redo them until the rest of the face is fully filled in."

CHAPTER 3

Designing Your Rug

The Orchard, 33" x 44", hand-cut and hand-dyed wool and cashmere on linen. Designed and hooked by Rachelle LeBlanc, St. Albert, Alberta, Canada, 2010. PHOTO COURTESY OF RACHELLE LEBLANC

Rachelle based this rug on a fleeting moment that she says "took my breath away while watching my girls."

You have many options to choose from as you design your hooked rug portrait. Do you want your portrait to be a view of the subject's face (called a "head shot" in the world of photography), or would you like to include other people in the final design? Do you want your subject to be facing you directly, looking off to the side, or in profile? Is your subject a person or an animal? Is the design something that is coming from your own imagination, or were you inspired by a photograph?

Designers of hooked rug portraits generally choose among three different styles: caricature, realistic, or impressionistic.

Caricature. A caricature shows you something about the subject by exaggerating features of the composition. Caricatures often have a cartoon-like quality. The rugs *If the Shoe Fits* by Suzanne Dirmaier, *Harry* by Diane Phillips, and *American Icon* by Rae Harrell exemplify this style.

Caricature designs are often drawn freehand, which is how Suzanne Dirmaier draws most of her designs. She says, "*If the Shoe Fits* was based on a dream I had. When I get an idea, I usually make a sketch, and if I am lucky, the final rug looks like the sketch."

ABOVE: *American Icon,* 25" x 17", #6- to 8-cut hand-dyed wool and hand-cut novelty fabrics on monk's cloth. Designed and hooked by Rae Harrell, Hinesburg, Vermont, 2006.

RIGHT: *Harry,* 15" x 19", #7-cut hand-dyed, over-dyed, and as-is wool on linen. Designed and hooked by Diane Phillips, Fairport, New York, 1998.

LEFT: *If the Shoe Fits,* 35" x 28", #8- and 4-cut hand-dyed wool on linen. Designed and hooked by Suzanne Dirmaier, Waterbury Center, Vermont, 2007.

According to Suzanne, "I don't do a lot of advance planning. My hooking is more of an organic experience. I have to work hard at hooking straight lines. I don't use dye formulas very much, and if I do, I change them with no chance of ever making the same color again. If I run out of a color of wool, I can find another that will do. (The plus side is that my dyeing mistakes yield great color choices for other rugs.) I am never sure if I want a border, or if I do, how big it will be. I just begin. My rugs change a lot from the time I have an idea to when the rug is finished. I want to be open to the possibilities that might dance across my frame."

Julie Rogers approached creating a family portrait from a unique perspective. Rather than hook images of people, blue jeans represent each member of the family as they were in 1998, the year this piece was completed. The largest belongs to her husband, Bill. The next size down is her pair. The smallest represent son Sam who was six, and the overalls were daughter Alita's at age three. Note how Julie's background is thematically appropriate to the composition. You would expect to see an outdoor view beyond a clothesline. Julie, however, did not concern herself with hooking the "real" view past the clothesline of her back yard. She edited the composition to omit many extraneous houses, including her own, leaving only the barn. The distant mountains and red barn tell a story about this family, suggesting they live in a rural community where old-fashioned traditions, such as hanging clothes on a wash line, still exist. Julie does. She lives in Vermont. Using this landscape as a background for her family portrait enhances the image.

Often, portraits are enhanced by the simplest of backgrounds. Here are some tips for designing the right background for your hooked rug portrait:

- "Less is more" when it comes to backgrounds for portraits.
- If you want to emphasize the facial expression, choose a background color that compliments the subject without distracting from it.
- If your face is depicted with both a light and dark side, hook your background so the transition from light to dark corresponds. For example, if a light source throws shadows on a face, it will throw corresponding shadows on a walled backdrop.
- Bold lines and lots of movement in the background can be confused with hair. Make sure, through use of value and directional hooking, that it is clear

where your subject's head ends and the background begins.
- If you add elements to the background, make sure they do not look like they are sprouting from your subject's head.
- The background can be an excellent place to pull together colors and textures. Use colors and fiber from other elements in your composition in the background.

- Add texture and movement to your background through directional hooking. For instance, if you use the same piece of flatly dyed wool for the entire background, try hooking it in swirls.
- Make sure there is enough contrast in value between the background and subject. Look at your piece from a distance to make sure you are getting this right.

Family Jeans, 40" x 26¹/₂", #8-cut hand-dyed and as-is wool on monk's cloth. Designed and hooked by Julie Rogers, Huntington, Vermont, 1998.

Paul Laurence Dunbar, 14½" x 36", #4- to 6-cut hand-dyed wool on linen. Designed and hooked by Donna Hrkman, Dayton, Ohio, 2009. From the collection of LaVerne Sci. PHOTO COURTESY OF DONNA HRKMAN

Paul Laurence Dunbar (1872–1906) was an internationally recognized poet whose parents escaped from slavery in Kentucky and settled in Ohio.

Realism. Realistic hooked rug portraits are often created with the help of photographs. Patty Yoder (1943–2005) hooked portraits of people and animals that are amazingly lifelike. She took multiple photographs of her subject until she found a composition that pleased her. The photo became the template for the design of her rug. She literally copied what she saw in the photo. Patty chose colors and values of wool that closely matched the colors and values represented in the original photograph. In her estimation, this type of rug design is easy because it requires one to make a minimum of artistic decisions. Both the composition and color planning come directly from the photo.

Subtle shading is an integral part of realism. It adds a three-dimensional quality to Donna Hrkman's work. For *Paul Laurence Dunbar,* she emphasized value rather than color. The entire rug is hooked from wool dyed using Cushing's Mahogany. "I was working from an old black-and-white photo but thought the warmer palette of a sepia-toned effect would be more appealing." Donna started with a half yard of wool. For each succeeding piece of lighter-valued wool, she used a half yard of wool and half the amount of dye as the previous batch. Donna repeated this method until she had seven values of light to dark. "I used the lightest shade, which was essentially natural wool, for his shirt and for highlights. The darkest value was used for his hair and shaded elements of his garments."

Donna always strives for realism in her representation, but also allows for artistic freedom. *Veterans Day* was

Veterans Day, 28½" x 35",
#4- to 6-cut hand-dyed wool
on linen. Designed and
hooked by Donna Hrkman,
Dayton, Ohio, 2010. PHOTO
COURTESY OF DONNA HRKMAN

inspired by a public domain photo. The original showed a gentleman named Mr. Ambrose standing with other people who were watching a parade. While she did not wish to include the other figures, she took a cue from their attire. They wore heavy topcoats, so Donna surmised the photo was taken on a cold day. "I reddened Mr. Ambrose's nose and ears, thinking he must have been very cold, standing in his old WWI uniform." His skin tones range from pale pink to the blue-gray of his veined hands.

Esther, 30" x 46", #4-cut hand-dyed wool on linen. Designed and hooked by Patty Yoder, Tinmouth, Vermont, 2001.

Ben and His Bass, 17½" x 17½", plied threads of silk, wool, cotton, rayon, polyester, etc., on woven cotton. Designed and hooked by Anne-Marie Littenberg, Burlington, Vermont, 2005.

The camera was an important tool for me when I designed *Ben and His Bass*. I wanted to capture a realistic image of my husband playing his five-stringed German instrument. I wanted the lines and proportions of Ben, his clothes, and his instrument to be precisely correct. However, I was not interested in matching colors, nor did I care to include all of the elements captured by my original photo. I eliminated a window at Ben's back, a pole lamp, and a set of drums visible in the original photo. The drape of his shirt, the wrinkles in his jeans, and the light reflecting on the instrument are copied exactly from the photo. In reality, only his shirt and jeans are blue. The walls are off-white; the bass, mahogany; the carpet, beige; and his skin, peachy beige.

Impressionism. With realism, accurate representation of the subject is of primary importance. With impressionism, the artistic vision, emotion, and sensibility of the artist may be emphasized over any precise rendering of the subject's physical characteristics. Impressionism is a popular style in hooked rug portraits. These portraits are often characterized by a free and creative use of color. Less concern is placed on accurate lines and proportion. Emphasis is placed on the overall visual effect of the composition rather

than fine detail. Color can be vibrant, and the rug hooker's personality and emotion may shine through. Designs are often spontaneous. Transition between colors of wool is abrupt, and shading is not necessarily subtle; in fact, shadows may be bold.

Diane Phillips usually designs her rugs as she hooks. She starts by drawing an elliptical shape on her backing. "Then I draw a circle inside the ellipse, and another circle inside that." These shapes become an eye and represent the extent of her sketching. "I take my wool and outline the eye, and then fill in the iris, pupil, and white of the eye. After the basic eye, I fill in shadows around the eye, thinking in terms of what protrudes on a face, and what recedes. I put lighter values where parts of the face protrude and darker where it recedes."

Look at anyone and notice that generally the top of someone's cheekbones and their brow bones are lighter because they protrude. The same is true for the top of a chin, and the plump part of the lower lip. Parts that recede include the eyelid fold, the shadow

Art Deco Woman, 17" x 20", #6- to 8-cut hand-dyed, over-dyed, and as-is wool on linen. Designed and hooked by Diane Phillips, Fairport, New York, 2009.

Nina, 25 1/2" x 30", #6-cut hand-dyed wool and novelty yarns (wool, acrylic, rayon, alpaca) on monk's cloth. Designed and hooked by Barbara Held, Tinmouth, Vermont, 2004.

under the nostrils, and the lines and wrinkles of age. For Diane, the rest of the face unfolds as she pulls her loops.

For *Nina,* Barbara Held began by drawing the shape of the head and the outlines of the eyes, nose, and mouth on her backing. She then began to spontaneously hook. For other portrait rugs, she first draws out detailed shapes representing the light and dark areas of the face. She generally starts by hooking the eyes. "I am never sure if I like how I have hooked the features until the face is done." Only after the face is fully hooked will she decide if areas need to be torn out and reworked. "With *Nina,* I just sort of hooked without thinking about it." This was Barbara's first portrait, and she says, "I have mixed feelings about the contrast." Barbara always hooks the hair last. "The shapes and colors for the hair form in my mind as I hook the face."

NY via IA, 26" x 27", #3- to 8-cut over-dyed and as-is wool on monk's cloth. Designed and hooked by Diane Learmonth, Anacortes, Washington, 2005. PHOTO COURTESY OF C. DENNIS MAYER

RIGHT: *New Liberty,* 13¼" x 17½", #7-cut hand-dyed, over-dyed, and as-is wool on linen. Designed and hooked by Diane Phillips, Fairport, New York, 2010.

Me, Before My Hair Turned Silver, 17¹/₂" x 29¹/₂", #6- to 8-cut hand-dyed wool on monk's cloth.
Designed and hooked by Gloria Reynolds Stokes, Hinesburg, Vermont, 2007.
Gloria copied one of her own original paintings.

ENHANCING YOUR HOOKED RUG PORTRAIT WITH ADDITIONAL ELEMENTS

What other elements should you include in your hooked rug portrait? To answer this question, you first have to figure out what your portrait rug is about. Diane Learmonth's *Rose* shows a woman whose intense gaze suggests any number of story lines. The strong colors and lines in her face are balanced by the simple, neutral background. Placing Rose against a heavily patterned background might have distracted the viewer's eye from the subject's expression.

Compare *Nina* with Jule Marie Smith's *Kaelin* (page 40), where the rug is about all of the other elements in addition to this piece's namesake. Kaelin, Jule's grand-

Rose, 15½" x 15½", #3- to 8-cut as-is and over-dyed wool on linen burlap. Designed and hooked by Diane Learmonth, Anacortes, Washington, 2007. PHOTO COURTESY OF C. DENNIS MAYER

Untitled, 10" x 11", #6- to 8-cut hand-dyed, over-dyed, and as-is wool on linen. Designed and hooked by Diane Phillips, Fairport, New York, 2009.

Kaelin, 85½" x 51½", hand-cut, hand-dyed wool on rug warp. Designed and hooked by Jule Marie Smith, Ballston Spa, New York, 2009. PHOTO COURTESY OF DAN SMITH

daughter, is only partially in view. It seems as if "all things K" are honored here. In Rae Harrell's *Every Moment* (page 42), the view of the face is so tightly framed that no room is left in the composition for anything

else. Contrast this design choice with *Kaelin*, where it may take a moment to realize a portrait of a little girl is hooked into the rug.

Sharon Townsend's *Journey* (page 43) is about multiple phases of her life as a young woman, wife and mother, and grandmother. While a self-

portrait, this rug isn't about Sharon's face. Thus, the facial features are depicted with great simplicity, and emphasis is placed on the surrounding elements, each of which holds personal meaning for Sharon and represents some aspect of her life.

Looking for Red Shoes by Suzanne Dirmaier shows how the portrait subject (her mother) and additional elements (boxes of red shoes) can be balanced so that both play vital roles in the composition. The array of individually unique and glamorous red shoes and the lady "of a certain age" framed by the orange settee are of equal importance in this composition. On their own, they might have some interest. But together in a single hooked rug, they tell a powerful tale.

Every Moment, 12" x 18", #6- to 8-cut hand-dyed wool on monk's cloth. Designed and hooked by Rae Harrell, Hinesburg, Vermont, 2006.

Looking for Red Shoes, 39" x 53", #6- and 8-cut hand-dyed wool on linen. Designed and hooked by Suzanne Dirmaier, Waterbury Center, Vermont, 2005.

Journey, 35" x 48", #6-cut hand-dyed wool on linen. Designed and hooked by Sharon Townsend, Altoona, Iowa, and Marathon, Florida, 2000. PHOTO COURTESY OF TOM TUSSEY

Digging Geoducks, 33" x 24", #5- to 7-cut hand-dyed and as-is wool on linen. Designed and hooked by Michele Wise, Seabeck, Washington, 2009. PHOTO COURTESY OF ERIC SCOUTEN

Blue, 24" x 26", hand-cut and hand-dyed wool and cashmere on linen. Designed and hooked by Rachelle LeBlanc, Montreal, Quebec, Canada, 2007. PHOTO COURTESY OF RACHELLE LEBLANC

Rachelle added drama to this self-portrait by cropping the head and elbows, giving the viewer a zoomed-in shot of the figure.

A hooked rug portrait can be more than a record of a person, face, or emotion. Sometimes, the portrait illustrates history, showing the subject engaged in a particular activity. Michele Wise lost her father over 30 years ago. She treasures an old black-and-white photo of him digging geoducks (a species of large saltwater clam) on Hood Canal, part of Puget Sound in the state of Washington. Michele wanted her rug to have more compositional impact than the original black-and-white photo, so she edited it, eliminating extra people, adding color, and elongating the perspective.

The Deportation, 32" x 43", hand-cut, hand-dyed wool and cashmere on linen. Designed and hooked by Rachelle LeBlanc, Montreal, Quebec, Canada, 2007. PHOTO COURTESY OF RACHELLE LEBLANC

  This rug commemorates the period between 1755 and 1762 when British authorities in Quebec stripped Acadians of their rights and placed them in the holds of overcrowded ships bound for destinations unknown. Rachelle's ancestors were among those Acadians.

Taking Possession, 38" x 48", hand-cut and hand-dyed wool and cashmere on linen. Designed and hooked by Rachelle LeBlanc, Montreal, Quebec, Canada, 2007. PHOTO COURTESY OF RACHELLE LEBLANC

"Francois and Charlitte LeBlanc, Acadians, found their way back home to Quebec following the great deportation. Legend has it that on June 24, 1785, they carved a cross into the bark of a large pine tree to mark their possession of the land that would later be called Bouctouche."

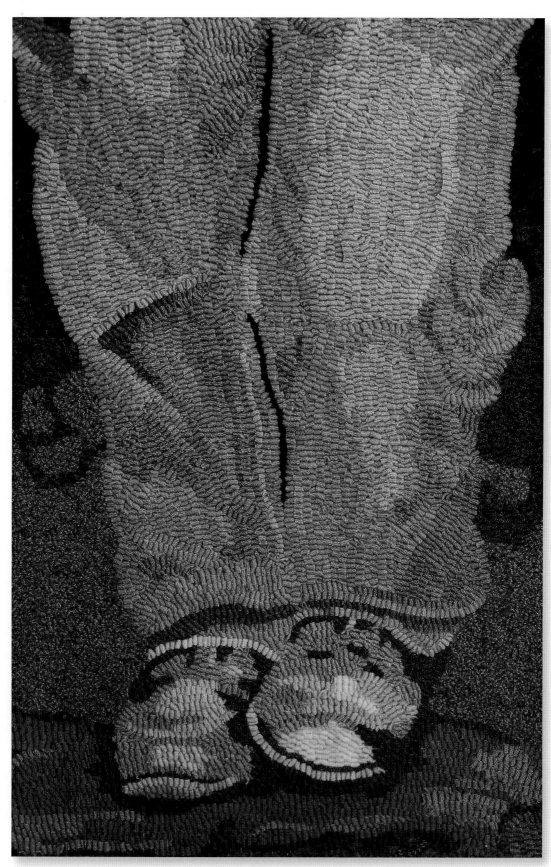

Steve Fish (jeans detail) by Patty Yoder. (See the full rug on page 53.) Four values of the same color blue were used to create blue jeans.

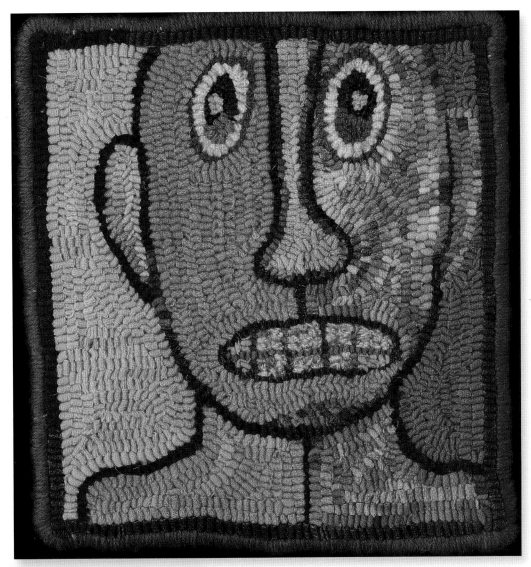

Untitled 2, 15" x 15½", #6- to 8-cut hand-dyed, over-dyed, and as-is wool on linen. Designed and hooked by Diane Phillips, Fairport, New York, 2007.

The Town Hooker, 31" x 42", #6-cut hand-torn, dyed, and as-is wool and nylon on linen. Designed and hooked by Wanda Kerr, Wiarton, Ontario, Canada, 2004.

Wanda says, "I wanted to make a joke, hooking a rug of me hooking a rug. I used a simple thought process to create this rug: I looked for shapes only, filling them in with the right value, temperature, and saturation of color." PHOTO COURTESY OF WANDA KERR

CHAPTER 4

Drawing
Your
Pattern

Some rug hookers are able to pick up a blank piece of backing, strips of wool, and a hook, and begin their design process by spontaneously hooking. And then there are those who prefer to plan in advance, making sketches and toying with ideas. An array of options exist when it's time to translate the idea for your design from your head to your backing.

The most important message I want to impart here is to encourage you to use whatever tools and tricks you can dream up to help you design, draw, and complete your rug. Most people do not have the technical skills to freehand draw a realistic animal or human face (especially if they have no formal training). And yet, many of those people create rugs with realistic looking characters. They use a wide array of tools to accomplish this task.

Artists have always used tools to help in the creation of their work. Caravaggio (1571–1610) painted people so precisely that when you see his paintings printed in black and white, they look like photographs. He and other Renaissance artists used a tool called a *camera lucida*, which projected the image they were trying to paint. They literally traced their figures onto their canvases. Vermeer (1632–1675) used a device called a *camera obscura* to project his images onto canvas. Norman Rockwell (1894–1978) used a film camera and projector for virtually all of his illustrations. He had people dress up in costume and pose for him with props. He photographed them extensively, then traced copies of his photos onto his canvas before he filled in the composition with paint. He was one of the great American illustrators of all time, and he, too, used tools. As soon as lenses were invented, artists found ways to use them to help copy their sub-

jects. I tell you this so you understand that almost no one is able to freehand sketch a perfect, photo-realistic image. Usually, freehand sketching produces images that are impressionistic or caricatures.

Grandsons, 36" x 24", #4-cut hand-dyed and as-is wool on monk's cloth. Designed and hooked by Ruth St. George, Shelburne, Vermont, 2008.

A photo of Ruth's grandsons, William (left) and Nicholas (right), was the basis for this rug. Jon Ciemiewicz helped her create the design by using an overhead projector, attaching the backing to the wall, projecting the photo, and tracing it.

The Cousins, 22½" x 17½",
#8-cut hand-dyed wool on
linen. Adapted from a family
photograph and drawn onto
the backing by Roslyn
Logsdon. Hooked by Diane
Kelly, Dorset, Vermont, 1994.

Diane says, "When it
comes to creating a hooked
portrait, I rely on photographs
for guidance. Photography
allows me to capture a
moment, a gesture, an
instance of attitude, or mood
that I like. I usually take a
tracing of a print to a photocopy store and have it
enlarged. I then trace the
enlargement onto red dot and
transfer it to linen. I do not try
to include detail, but just the
basic outline, and save the
detail for wool color and
directional hooking."

You can use a variety of methods to draw your design on your backing.

Sketch. You can take a soft pencil, piece of charcoal, or tailor's chalk and begin sketching directly on your backing. Charcoal, chalk, and pencil are convenient in that mistakes can be rubbed out and redrawn. However, their impermanence can be a hindrance when you begin to hook and the movement of your hands and wool across the backing erases lines you want to keep. If you initially use charcoal, chalk, or pencil to draw directly on your backing, go over your lines again with a permanent black marker. (Note that permanent markers in colors other than black are generally not really permanent.)

I use this method when designing rugs, often just laying down a few basic lines before I begin my hooking. When I do this, however, I have generally first done a number of initial sketches on inexpensive pads made of newsprint paper. I practice my layout and design a number of times before marking up my backing. I use this method to create a piece that is impressionistic, abstract, or a caricature.

Camera, photocopies, and red dot transfer material. How can you transfer a design based on a photograph to your backing so the resulting image is realistic? Patty Yoder used a camera, photocopier, and red dot transfer material when designing her rugs. After photographing her subject, Patty printed the photo in standard snapshot size. Her next step was to place the photo on a light box, and lay a piece of tracing paper over it. She traced as much detail as she wanted onto the tracing paper, resulting in a 4" by 6" initial sketch. Patty excluded details from her tracing that she felt were not compositionally

Steve Fish, 33$\frac{1}{2}$" x 63$\frac{1}{2}$", #4-cut hand-dyed wool on linen. Designed and hooked by Patty Yoder, Tinmouth, Vermont, 2003.

Patty copied a photo she took of Steve standing in the doorway of a barn. The bovine rump was added to the composition later.

Precious, 29" x 24", #6-cut wool strips, yarn, and nylon on linen. Designed and hooked by Wanda Kerr, Wiarton, Ontario, Canada, 2004. PHOTO COURTESY OF WANDA KERR

Wanda designed this rug to include a person (her daughter) and an animal because "of the fuss people make over hooking animals. I see no difference between hooking faces in fur versus skin. With both, I look for shapes and color. If the shapes are correct, it doesn't matter which way you hook them. I remember hooking her eyebrows first and being thrilled by how much they took the shape of my daughter's. If I hook someone I know, I want them to be identifiable; I want their spirit and passion to be read by the viewer."

Angus, 62" x 42", hand- and commercially dyed one- and two-ply, bulky and fine, straight spun and bouclé yarns (wool, mohair, silk, and angora), and roving on linen. Designed and hooked by Heidi Wulfraat, Lakeburn, New Brunswick, Canada, 2008. PHOTO COURTESY OF HEIDI WULFRAAT

Angus, a Newfoundland, is Heidi's constant companion. This scene is located along the shore in Rock Port, New Brunswick. When designing rugs, Heidi surrounds herself with photos of the subject matter and setting. She draws the design freehand using a light-colored permanent marker pen and makes adjustments with darker colors. Working freehand makes it easy for Heidi to work in a very large scale.

R Is for Ramsey, a Gentle Shepherd, 35" x 50", #4-cut hand-dyed wool on linen. Designed and hooked by Patty Yoder, Tinmouth, Vermont, 1994.

Aloha, 9½" x 10½", #6- to 8-cut hand-dyed, over-dyed, and as-is wool on linen. Designed and hooked by Diane Phillips, Fairport, New York, 2009.

Diane begins many of her rugs by drawing a single eye on the backing and then hooking it. The face and personality emerge as the rug is completed. She rarely draws an entire design on the backing or makes advance sketches.

important to the final image. However, she paid very close attention to the subtle shadows seen on faces, fur, and textiles.

She then took the traced sketch to a local photocopying store where it was blown up and reproduced in whatever size Patty wanted for her hooked rug design. Using a permanent marking pen in black, Patty went over the lines of the enlarged photocopy, outlining the shape of every shadow and element she wished to include. Finally, she used red dot pattern transfer material to get her detailed sketch on her backing. The photograph (her original source material) was always at hand, a vital visual aid, as she picked up her hook and started pulling loops. Patty chose colors and values of wool that closely matched the colors and values in the original photograph.

In Patty's estimation, this type of rug design is easy because it required her to make a minimum of artistic decisions. Both the composition and color planning came directly from the photo.

Alluminia, 16³/₄" x 16",
hand-cut, hand-dyed wool
on rug warp. Designed and
hooked by Jule Marie Smith,
Ballston Spa, New York,
2004.

Transfer pen or pencil. An alternative to red dot transfer material is a pattern-transfer pen or pencil. Make a tracing of your photograph and enlarge it to the desired size. Lay an additional piece of tracing paper over the enlargement. Make a pencil tracing of the image. Then, go over every pencil line with a pattern-transfer pen or pencil. Lay your backing flat on a hard surface that can take the heat of an iron. Lay your traced copy face down so the transfer pen or pencil marks are facing the backing. Follow the instructions that come with the transfer pen or pencil, and iron your image onto the backing. Keep in mind this technique will produce a mirror image of your original picture.

Light table. A light table large enough to hold your pattern is another alternative. Once you have an enlargement of your original photo, trace the lines you want to copy with a permanent marker to darken them. Lay the enlargement face up on the light table. Lay your backing over the enlargement, turn on the light, and begin tracing with a pencil. It helps to use masking tape to secure the corners of both the enlargement and backing before you trace your image. When you have made a complete tracing with

T Is for Toby, the First Lamb to Come to the Farm, 50" x 31", #4-cut hand-dyed wool on linen. Designed and hooked by Patty Yoder, Tinmouth, Vermont, 1995. This self-portrait shows Patty holding Toby.

pencil, go over all the lines on the backing one more time with a black permanent marker.

Projectors. Take a tip from Vermeer and project your design onto the backing. Secure your blank backing to the wall. Using an overhead or slide projector, project your image onto your backing. Use a pencil or charcoal to trace the projection onto your backing. When the entire design is traced, go back over it with a permanent marker.

The grid method. Donna Hrkman used the grid method, combined with freehand drawing, in designing her rug, *Paul Laurence Dunbar.*

Clouded Leopard, 18" x 24", #4-cut hand-dyed wool on linen. Designed and hooked by Jon Ciemiewicz, Hudson, New Hampshire, 2009. PHOTO COURTESY OF JON CIEMIEWICZ

Inspired by a photo of a leopard in a zoo in Bangkok (where he was once stationed), Jon hand-drew this image. According to Jon, "The cat is approximately life size. Clouded leopards are native to southeast Asia. Wild cats are one of my loves."

(Her article in the January/February 2009 issue of *Rug Hooking* magazine, titled "Gridded Landscapes," provides a detailed overview of this method.) Start by making a copy of the photo you wish to use as your hooked rug portrait design (the copy will allow you to mark up the picture without ruining your original). Draw a grid on the photo, using precise lines so each square is exactly the same size. For a 7" by 11" photo, make a grid using 1" squares. This process will give you a grid with 10 evenly spaced horizontal lines and 7 evenly spaced vertical lines on your photo. Next, decide what size you want your rug to be. Mark the rug's outer edges on your backing (for this example, let's say it is 28" by 44"). Now, lightly draw a grid on the backing, evenly spacing your horizontal and vertical lines so you end up with the exact same number of evenly spaced grid lines that you drew on your photograph. The next step is to start drawing the design. Match a square on your original photo with the corre-

Daphne, 52" x 76", hand-cut, hand-dyed wool on rug warp. Designed and hooked by Jule Marie Smith, Ballston Spa, New York, 2009. The figure of Daphne was drawn freehand. Jule used a life model (me) to get the position of the lifted leg correct. The foliage, earth, splashing river, and background were hooked from Jule's imagination directly onto the backing, without preliminary sketches.

Daphne (face detail) by Jule Marie Smith. Notice all the different colors used for Daphne's complexion.

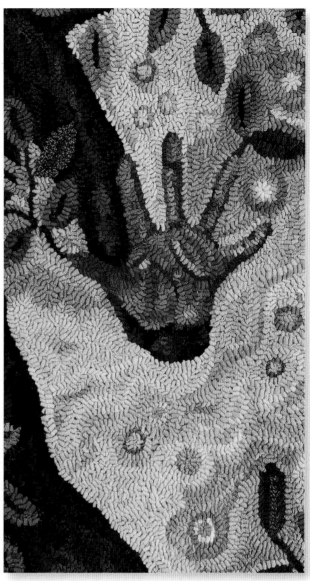

Daphne (hand detail) by Jule Marie Smith. Although the colors are fantastic, the shape and the lines in the hand are realistic.

sponding square on the backing. (You may want to number your horizontal rows and alphabetically mark your vertical rows to make is easier to find corresponding grid points on your backing. Then, as you would with a road map, you can focus on area A5 or D2, easily identifying corresponding points on both grids.) Carefully draw that square's contents on the backing. Do not focus on the entire composition; it will be overwhelming. Just focus on each little square, one at a time. This tried-and-true method of copying has been successfully used for centuries. You can find additional detailed instructions by using an Internet search engine and looking up the phrase "grid method drawing."

You can buy software for your computer that will convert any digital image into a "paint by numbers" style pattern. These programs also provide you with the corresponding color key. Look for a software application that is compatible with your computer. The software will allow you to choose a color palette and preview the image in your color selection. Once you have printed your pattern, take it to a photocopy store and enlarge it. Use any of the methods described above to transfer it to your backing.

FINDING IMAGES

Public domain images. How can you find images of elements to copy for your composition, using any of the above methods, without violating copyright rules? Take out your camera and snap photos of the elements you wish to include in your composition: fauna and flora,

Mr. Bean and Me, 19³/₄" x 12¹/₂", #3- to 8-cut as-is and over-dyed wool on linen burlap. Designed and hooked by Diane Learmonth, Anacortes, Washington, 2009. PHOTO COURTESY OF C. DENNIS MAYER

Diane is a McGown-trained rug hooker who loves to work with high contrast, complementary colors. "I don't care what color it is as long as it works," she says, preferring to work in a bright palette. Her rugs are often inspired by her own photographs. She wants the resulting rug to resemble the photo in terms of placement of key elements, but she omits extraneous details. The camera is an essential design tool for Diane and she takes lots of photos. She prefers to leave her mistakes as they are, applying any lessons learned to her next rug. She is not interested in tearing out and re-hooking.

PUBLIC DOMAIN

Public domain images are an excellent source when you want to copy an item and include it in your design because you can do so without worrying about violating copyright law. You cannot use another's design to create your own design without that artist's permission, unless the image is in the public domain.

An image is in the public domain if it is 70 or more years past the date of the death of the original artist or if the image has been released to the public domain by whoever holds the copyright. If you copy someone else's work that is not in the public domain, and use it in your work, you may be violating copyright laws.

buildings, mountains, and so on. Another option is to go to the library or bookstore and find books that include public domain images. Because these images are in the public domain, you may use them in any way you wish without having to worry about violating copyright rules. Perhaps the easiest resource for finding public domain images is the Internet. Looking for a public domain image of a giraffe? Type into your search engine the phrase "public domain giraffe pictures." The result will be many websites offering free images of giraffes.

FROM YOUR OWN HAND

"I can't draw" is a phrase I hear constantly when I teach. But of course, if you can't draw, learn using the tried-and-true method of practice, practice, practice. Get yourself a sketch pad and just play with pencil, charcoal, pastel, and other drawing mediums. Read books on the subject. Be fearless.

CHAPTER 5

Adults and Children

London Bridge, 32" x 38", hand-cut and hand-dyed wool and cashmere on linen. Designed and hooked by Rachelle LeBlanc, St. Albert, Alberta, Canada, 2009. From a series titled "Fleeting Moments." PHOTO COURTESY OF RACHELLE LEBLANC

When hooking young versus older figures, a number of design elements must be considered. The most obvious details are gray hair and wrinkles for the older figures. Another could be the activity engaging your subject. Adults are unlikely to play "London Bridge," as the figures do in Rachelle LeBlanc's rug of that title.

Foster and the Boys, 17" x 23", #3- and 4-cut hand-dyed and as-is wool on linen. Designed and hooked by Suzanne Dirmaier, Waterbury Center, Vermont, 1998.

This rug depicts the daily scene at the Davis General Store in Albany, Vermont, circa 1970. The man at the far right is Suzanne's grandfather. She says, "I chose to do this piece in memory of my grandfather and because I was struck by the rituals of men that often are overlooked. These men met daily at the general store and gossiped, talked politics, weather, etc., in much the same way women met over other activities. Although these men are now all dead and the store burned down, they remain in my memory."

Too Much Yin and Not Enough Yang, 27" x 28", #6- to 8-cut hand-dyed wool with ribbed knit appliqué on linen. Designed and hooked by Rae Harrell, Hinesburg, Vermont, 2007.

Adults carry themselves differently than children. Is there any doubt the figures in *Foster and the Boys* by Suzanne Dirmaier are grown men? Other cues come from details such as the broom and cane in the hands of two figures.

What a figure is wearing can also give clues about age. Rosy lipstick and blue eye shadow suggest a grown woman in Rae Harrell's *Too Much Yin and Not Enough Yang*. The difference seems obvious when you contrast young and old in a single portrait, as Laura Pierce did in *Will and Kirby*, showing differences in size, a gently thinning pate, and facial hair.

One way to age a face is to use less contrast in outlining eyes and lips, defining cheeks, and hooking hair. Think of the way a woman applies makeup to help her look more fresh and youthful: she enhances the dark lines that outline her eyes (with mascara and eye shadow), eyebrows, lips, and pink cheeks. Also, as we age, there is less contrast between our graying hair and skin tones; it is as if everything transitions to a middle value. Vibrantly colored hair is a symbol of youth.

Will and Kirby, 16" x 20", #3- and 8-cut hand-dyed and as-is wool on linen. Designed and hooked by Laura Pierce, Petaluma, California, 2005. PHOTO COURTESY OF LAURA PIERCE

According to Laura, "Most of my portraits are designed from photographs. Since rug hooking is a chunkier medium than photography, only the essential elements can be translated into hooking. Our color palette is also much more limited. A translation takes place between photo and rug, and one hopes there is a resemblance when the piece is finished."

Katharine, 15" x 16", #4- to 6-cut as-is and hand-dyed wool on monk's cloth. Designed and hooked by Barbara Held, Tinmouth, Vermont, 2004.

Diane Phillips ages her subjects' faces by adding lines around the mouth, bags under the eyes, and wrinkles on the forehead. "It takes about six lines to age a person by 20 to 30 years in a hooked rug portrait," she says. In addition, facial proportions are different in older subjects. "Older people tend to have larger features. One's ears and nose never stop growing. Skin drags, especially on necks."

HOOKING SPECIFIC FEATURES

Diane Phillips cautions rug hookers against rehooking too early in the process. She says, "One challenge of hooking faces is you begin with the eyes and nose, and they seem enormous until the rest of the face has been hooked in; the features look twice the size they should be. Resist the urge to tear them out. Study your progress by looking at the back of your rug. It will give you a more accurate sense of how the final proportions will work out. Everything becomes more balanced when the entire face is hooked."

Mouth. The upper lip is generally darker than the lower lip because it is in shadow. Light is often reflected off the plump part of the lower lip, suggesting a pout. Placement of dark lines at the corners of the mouth can help convey a sense of mood. Note the little hollow under the bottom lip, at the top of the chin. Forgetting a

Hooking the portrait of a child presents unique challenges. I find many painted portraits of children to be odd. Faces can lose their animation, and postures are often too adult. I have seen portraits where the expression is too adult-like, even if the proportions are accurate. Sometimes these portraits look more like dolls than children. In addition, while designing and hooking a portrait of an "interesting" looking adult can be intriguing, in children, any oddness just looks creepily and sadly strange. We may be intrigued by seeing a wide range of "experience" in an adult's face. In a child's, we look for fresh innocence, expectation, and joy.

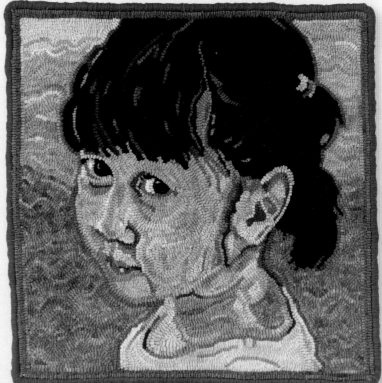

Sunshine Girl, 16" x 16", #4- and 6-cut hand-dyed wool on linen. Designed and hooked by Donna Hrkman, Dayton, Ohio, 2008. PHOTO COURTESY OF DONNA HRKMAN

Based on a photo Donna took of her niece, Jessamy. She used the grid method for transferring the design to her backing to minimize distortion of the face design. Warm colors and subtle transition between values are the keys to hooking a child's face that glows with good health. Note the very light line outlining the bridge of the nose and the glint on Jessamy's lower lip.

- Children are pert, with higher foreheads and rounder faces than adults.
- Babies' heads are large in proportion to the size of their faces and bodies, even though their heads are less than half the size of adults'.
- A newborn's length measures about $3\frac{1}{2}$ times the size of their head. Their legs are short, and they have prominent bellies and long torsos.
- By age three, a child's height measures about 5 times their head size.
- A baby's face covers about $\frac{1}{3}$ the size of her cranial mass, while an adult's covers about half.
- A baby's nose and mouth are about the same width as one of her eyes.
- Toddlers have full, round cheeks and tiny chins.
- While the proportion of most children's features varies dramatically from adults, the size of the iris is always about the same as an adult's. This is why children's eyes seem so large.
- As a child ages, the jaw gets larger, eyebrows darken, and hair thickens.
- Proportions become similar to adults' during the early teens.
- You see more of the white of the child's eye as she ages. Also, the mouth is further from the bottom of the chin as the jaw develops, and the nose grows longer.
- Use warm pastels for the skin tone, and gentle transitions between values. (Blue and grey might make the image look like he or she is ill. Dramatic transition between values in the lines of the face will suggest age.)
- Use whimsy and humor in the design of other elements of the composition of children's portraits. When hooking adults, be more cautious about this because what can appear charming in the portrayal of a child can seem strange in an adult.

Secrets, 15" x 15", #6- to 8-cut hand-dyed, over-dyed, and as-is wool on linen. Designed and hooked by Diane Phillips, Fairport, New York, 2005.

Diane Phillips says, "Part of the fun of hooking faces is I don't have a lot of expectation about what the piece will look like when it is done. I let it look like whatever it turns out to be. This is very different from someone who wants their portrait to look like an existing photograph. I try to encourage people hooking faces for the first time to begin with an image they make up in their head. If they start with the picture of someone they love, the pleasure in the hooking can be challenged by the difficulty in making an exact copy. It's better to start with something that doesn't have so much emotional baggage."

simple feature like this can make your rendering of a face less than realistic.

Keep the mouth simple. If you draw perfectly shaped lips, make sure the result does not make the face resemble a cartoon or commercial drawing for a cosmetics advertisement. Outlining the lips exaggerates a cartoon-like quality. Instead, indicate the mouth using a number of different values. Pay attention to the line that separates the upper and lower lips. Its position can indicate a great deal of expression.

Teeth. Teeth can be an enormous challenge. Take care when copying a photo that shows a smiling subject

exposing his or her pearly whites. When you begin hooking, you may find it very difficult to portray the teeth in a way that looks natural and not sinister. My solution is to recompose the view and not show teeth. Ruth St. George, however, had good success showing teeth in her rug *Grandsons.* Note the teeth are not pure white, and she uses a light value also used in other areas of the rug. In addition, she chose relatively light values for the shadows inside the mouth. In reality, the inside shadows of one's mouth appear almost black; however, this color would not have translated well to hooking.

Grandsons (detail) by Ruth St. George. Note the teeth are not pure white. Ruth used a light value taken from other areas of the rug. In addition, she used relatively light values for the shadows inside the mouth. (See the full rug on page 51.)

Nose. The nose sometimes casts a shadow across the eye. The nose is generally shaped like a wedge. The bone forms a narrow, flat plane that gets wider as it moves from between the eyes to the tip. The nostrils are like wings fanning out from the bone. The top plane of the nose catches some light, and the tip of the nose is also highlighted. The nostrils lie in deep shadow.

Neck. Light and shadow will determine how you see the neck. Use darker values to differentiate the jaw from the neck. The neck lies in the shadow of the jaw, and the hollow at the base of the neck can be indicated with a subtle shift in value. Men have an Adam's apple, and their necks tend to be thicker than women's.

Eyes. The upper lid of the eye slightly overlaps the top of the iris. The pupil can be indicated with one hooked loop flanked by two tails. You can make the bottom half of the iris a little bit lighter in value than the top, which appears darker because it lies in the shadow of the lashes.

Diane Phillips recommends holding off on placing a glint, that sparkle or highlighted spot in the iris, until the rest of the eye is complete. "The glint is what makes the face seem to come alive. The glint helps communicate happiness, relaxation, or focus, depending on where you put it and how dispersed you make it seem. If you place it on the edge of the pupil and iris, the subject seems much more relaxed than if you place it dead center, which reads as an intense glare. Thready wool with a loose weave in a small cut is excellent for hooking eyes.

Emma, 11" x 14", #8-cut hand-dyed and as-is wool on linen. Designed and hooked by Laura Pierce, Petaluma, California, 2009. PHOTO COURTESY OF LAURA PIERCE

Laura says, "I like to use the scrap bag, sorted by values of skin tones. Purples and greens make good shadows. It never hurts to have leftovers from a previous portrait project. I also dye 'skin' swatches so I have some good values to go with everything else. For hair, textured wool really helps with shadows and outlines." Laura was inspired by a photo she took of her mother, Emma, who is also an extraordinary rug hooker. Note the use of patterned rectangles as a background. They are reminiscent of rugs hooked by Emma. Touches of colors from Emma and her clothes are repeated in the background.

Also, hook your loops low and loose to achieve a blurry effect. You want the eyes to seem to recede into the head. If you hook crisp, prominent loops, the face will appear as if it has an odd medical condition."

Hair. Hooking hair allows for a lot of creative freedom. You can delineate individual strands to show off curl and wave. Remember that white hair is never really white, and black is never purely black. Dark blue is an excellent choice for

Little Mabel, 15" x 20", #3- and 4-cut hand-dyed and as-is wool on linen. Designed and hooked by Laura Pierce, Petaluma, California, 2003. PHOTO COURTESY OF LAURA PIERCE

The design for this rug was inspired by a sepia photo of Laura's grandmother, taken by Laura's great-grandmother in 1892.

Strong Woman (detail) by Priscilla Heininger. Priscilla used color blocking for wavy hair. (See the full rug on page 113).

adding highlights to black hair. Try choosing three different values: light, medium, and dark. Start with your darkest strips and hook in prominent lines and curls. Next, working with your lightest value, hook this wool next to the dark values to exaggerate contrast. Fill in the rest of the area with the medium value wool. Hair grows off the head in a circular pattern, so hook in the direction of the flow of the hair shaft.

Step back a good distance from your piece, and look at it with a squint. From a distance, can you still distinguish between the values of the hair strands? If they all seem the same in value, or have blurred into a single color, consider using higher contrast in your wool selection. Also, choose colors from other elements in your composition and place them in the hair. This placement will help balance color and texture in the overall piece.

Diane Phillips suggests using a higher, looser loop for hair. "I like wild hair. Textures and tweeds, anything bright and plaid, make excellent hair. Save those bits that you think are way too ugly to hook with."

La Vie en Rose, 38" x 32", hand-cut and hand-dyed wool and cashmere on linen. Designed and hooked by Rachelle LeBlanc, St. Albert, Alberta, Canada, 2010. PHOTO COURTESY OF RACHELLE LEBLANC

Part of Rachelle's "Fleeting Moments" series, *La Vie en Rose* translates as "life in shades of pink" or "looking at life through rose-colored glasses." Note how only one child is shown in full. The view of two additional figures is cropped, adding drama and interest to the composition. The background is hooked with the same colors and values as the dresses. Elements are distinct because of directional hooking and subtle use of outlining.

Profiles. A face in profile shows a different perspective on the features.

- The visible eye in a profile is recessed from the bridge of the nose. The front edge of the eye lines up with the outer edge of the lip.
- The forehead slopes in a bit from the brow to the hairline.
- The nose is prominent, even if someone has a small nose.

- The bottom of the lower lip lines up with the point of the jaw where the bone turns up toward the ear.
- The outside edge of the eyebrow lines up close to where the chin intersects with the neck.
- The top of the ear lines up with the bottom of the eyebrow.
- The neck has a slant. It is not perpendicular to the floor.

Mirror, Mirror, On the Wall, I Am My Mother After All, 29" x 32", #6- to 8-cut hand-dyed and as-is wool on linen. Designed and hooked by Suzanne Dirmaier, Waterbury Center, Vermont, 2002.

Note how hair color and style are all that is needed to suggest one person is older than another. Directional hooking and good contrast allow the viewer to distinguish individual strands of hair.

Cupcakes on Sunday Afternoon, 25" x 24", hand-cut, dyed wool and cashmere on linen. Designed and hooked by Rachelle LeBlanc, St. Albert, Alberta, Canada, 2010. From the collection of Roxanne Lullo. PHOTO COURTESY OF RACHELLE LEBLANC

The subject and composition of this rug were inspired by a black-and-white photograph of Roxanne as a child.

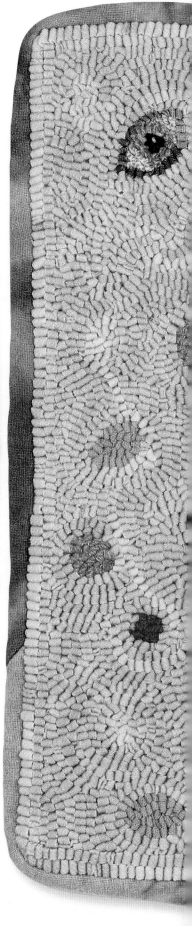

The Almost Virgin Queen, 34" x 40", #6-cut hand-dyed and as-is wool on linen. Designed and hooked by Pat Merikallio, Capitola, California, 2002. PHOTO COURTESY OF PHYLLIS FORD

For this self-portrait Pat says, "I like to use my leftover cut wool in the hooking, and I like to focus on values of many colors for my shading (skin, hair, everywhere) because I think it looks more interesting."

Where Did I Go? 18" x 18¹⁄₂", #8-cut hand-dyed wool on linen. Designed and hooked by Sharon Townsend, Altoona, Iowa, and Marathon, Florida, 2005. PHOTO COURTESY OF TOM TUSSEY

Sharon was inspired by Modigliani's (1884–1920) long-necked women in this piece about dementia. Sharon tells the story of her life and family through her hooked rug portraits.

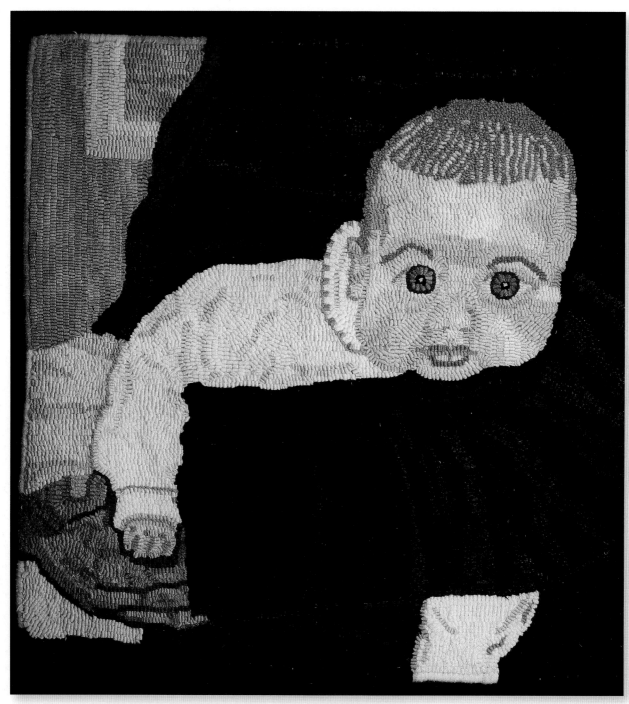

Baby Katie in Daddy's Arms, 22½" x 23", #6- to 8-cut hand-dyed wool on linen. Designed and hooked by Diane Kelly, Dorset, Vermont, 2007.

Diane says, "A photo of our son Paul, holding his daughter, Katie, reminded me of a painting by Edouard Manet (1832–1883). Manet painted his subjects with luminous skin, often framed by dark, almost black hair. I enlarged a tracing of the photograph, transferred it to linen, and began hooking Katie's face. Another artist I admire is rug hooker Pat Merikallio. Her portraits of children are wonderful, and as I studied them and the paintings of Mary Cassatt (1844–1926), I realized how many pastel colors could be used to create the wonder of a baby's flesh. I used pinks and peaches and then lilac for shadows. Paul's sweater was black velour, so I cut some black velour and tried hooking it. It was a disaster and shed all over the light face colors. I went back to wool and discovered that black can also be made up of many colors. The purple highlights and directional hooking created the folds of the sweater."

Katie: Let's Play, 13½" x 26", #6-cut hand-dyed and as-is wool with feather embellishment on linen. Designed and hooked by Diane Kelly, Dorset, Vermont, 2004.

LEFT: *Marcella,* 28" x 12", #3- to 6-cut hand-dyed wool and hand-cut novelty fabric on linen. Designed and hooked by Molly Dye, Jacksonville, Vermont, 2005. **RIGHT:** *Walter,* 11" x 28", #3- to 6-cut hand-dyed wool and hand-cut novelty fabrics on linen. Designed and hooked by Molly Dye, Jacksonville, Vermont, 2004. Walter is Molly's grandson, shown here ready to play with his tools. Granddaughter Marcella had a toy power saw, and the interaction inspired this rug.

A Cloudy Day at the Beach, 24" x 26", hand-cut, hand-dyed wool and cashmere on linen. Designed and hooked by Rachelle LeBlanc, Montreal, Quebec, Canada, 2007. PHOTO COURTESY OF RACHELLE LEBLANC

Rachelle says, "This is inspired by the disappointment my daughter felt after arriving at the beach and finding it closed due to dangerously high waves during a vacation in New Brunswick, Canada." The little girl's posture in this rug tells the story of her disappointment.

Still Winning, 38" x 46", #8-cut hand-dyed wool on linen. Designed and hooked by Sharon Townsend, Altoona, Iowa, and Marathon, Florida, 2005. PHOTO COURTESY OF TOM TUSSEY

Sharon says, "Mother was hospitalized, and because of her age, 91, there was discussion about whether to let her die comfortably. I was for operating. Two days later she was sitting up and playing cards. She lived three more years. The border design was inspired by pictures of a wallpaper design made in 1913, the year she was born. No one really likes this rug, but I love her spirit and wanted to try and express it in my art."

CHAPTER 6

Self-Portraits

Self Portrait Color Study (with brown hair), 14" x 14", #8-cut hand-dyed wool on linen. Designed and hooked by Diane Kelly, Dorset, Vermont, 2004.

How do you see yourself? How do you appear to the rest of the world? Listen to others describe themselves, and you may be struck by how you and they see things differently. Have you ever seen a photo of yourself that someone else thinks is an accurate representation, but which, to you, is a complete surprise or bears little resemblance?

Exploring our own appearance can be challenging. One tends to hear many self-deprecating comments when listening to someone talk about his or her own appearance. Even a simple compliment of, "You look nice," seems too often to be met with a response of, "I am too fat," or "I look terrible." This phenomenon makes the concept of self-portraits very interesting. How much are we willing to reveal by what we choose to portray?

Self Portrait Color Study (with blue hair), 14" x 14", #8-cut hand-dyed wool on linen. Designed and hooked by Diane Kelly, Dorset, Vermont, 2005.

Verbs of Growth, 26" x 20", #6- to 8-cut hand-dyed wool on linen. Designed and hooked by Diane Kelly, Dorset, Vermont, 2004.

What other design elements might we include to represent important personal aspects of our lives?

When Diane Kelly is planning a new design, she goes off by herself to think, assuming a quiet pose with eyes closed, her bent head resting on her hand. Her husband, Paul, photographed Diane one day as she sat deep in thought. Intrigued by the pose, Diane transferred the image to her backing and it became the basis for two interpretations, done about six months apart. Diane says, "They represent pre- and post-cataract surgery. So much clear color flooded into my life after cataract surgery that I wanted to try a more adventuresome portrait." She strove for realistic hair and skin tones in her first attempt. In the second, she freed herself from worrying about natural colors and focused on color value (qualities of light, medium, and dark) instead. Diane is a writer with a distinguished career in journalism. She says she designed *Verbs of Growth* when she "was still dependent on words" to get her thoughts across.

Sharon Townsend has designed and hooked many rugs depicting herself in a variety of moods, situations, and appearances. Her styles of self-portraits range from realism to caricature to impressionistic. A common denominator in them is that the self-portraits display qualities and elements about her personal appearance that anyone who knows her would recognize. These elements might be as simple as her silver hair and eyeglasses in *Study War No More* (page 86), *Wildflower/Moving On*, and *Checking the Corners* (page 85). (You can also identify these features in the portrait Diane Learmonth did of Sharon, *My Mentors*, page 86.) The identifiable qualities may be as subtle as her facial expressions in *Glorious Grammy* (page 84) and *Uncharted Waters* (page 87). Each piece represents a fearless quality about Sharon—one in which she pursues her vision and self-expression without concern for trying to glamorize her appearance or worry about anyone else's approval.

Wildflower, 50" x 29", and *Moving On,* 25" x 29", #8-cut hand-dyed wool on linen. Designed and hooked by Sharon Townsend, Altoona, Iowa, and Marathon, Florida, 2003. PHOTO COURTESY OF TOM TUSSEY

LEFT: *Glorious Grammy,* 30" x 48", #8-cut hand-dyed wool on linen. Designed and hooked by Sharon Townsend, Altoona, Iowa, and Marathon, Florida, 2000. PHOTO COURTESY OF TOM TUSSEY

Sharon says, "You must realize I am a lady of my generation, and going around nude or even drawing myself nude was quite an adventurous step for me. This proved to be the most freeing rug I had ever done—on so many levels. Once you step out there and decide you don't care what anyone thinks…well, you know the rest: FREEDOM." Sharon studied herself in the mirror, noting the lines, shapes, and positions of her body. "This could have been a serious problem what with my prude thinking. I hooked the body on the diagonal because I was inspired by watercolor paintings of women." The ginkgo leaf represents an ancient tree. Sharon included pearls because they helped show motion. "I got a pearl necklace the next Christmas from Bob [Sharon's late husband]. *Glorious Grammy* hangs in the entry to our home and not all the family is thrilled."

Checking the Corners, 14" x 15", #8-cut hand-dyed wool on linen. Designed and hooked by Sharon Townsend, Altoona, Iowa, and Marathon, Florida, 2005. PHOTO COURTESY OF TOM TUSSEY

After unexpectedly finding snakes where they shouldn't be, Sharon spent a few days walking through her home, checking the corners. "It occurred to me that while we are checking the corners in life, sometimes things are happening even closer to us."

Study War No More, 22" x 28", #8-cut hand-dyed wool on linen. Designed and hooked by Sharon Townsend, Altoona, Iowa, and Marathon, Florida, 2003. PHOTO COURTESY OF TOM TUSSEY

Flamingos are a common thematic element in Sharon's rugs. She saw a news report about flamingos in Iraq that had been captured and hitched together by a peddler trying to sell them to Kurds, who had themselves just been displaced from their own natural wetland area to the desert. This incident occurred just before the start of the Iraq war. Sharon wanted to express her anger in this self-portrait.

My Mentors, 30³/₄" x 15¹/₂", #3- to 8-cut as-is and over-dyed wool on monk's cloth. Designed and hooked by Diane Learmonth, Anacortes, Washington, 2006. PHOTO COURTESY OF C. DENNIS MAYER

Diane hooked portraits of (from left to right) Sharon Townsend, Dori Byer, and Lois Egenes.

Uncharted Waters, 32" x 38", #8-cut hand-dyed wool on linen. Designed and hooked by Sharon Townsend, Altoona, Iowa, and Marathon, Florida, 2005. Custom-made frame by Jim Lilly. PHOTO COURTESY OF TOM TUSSEY

    Sharon started with a blank backing, measured her features, and tripled the size of each. She used wool at hand, focusing on value rather than color. "The portrait hangs on the stone wall in our kitchen and the children say it has a look they remember from their childhood and they wish I would smile."

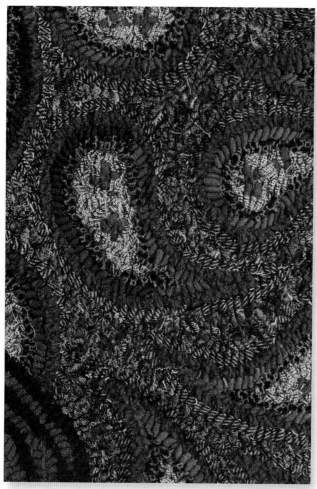

I Dream in Paisley (detail) by Rae Harrell. The paisley pattern was hooked with antique, paisley-patterned wool challis. When hooking with challis, hand cut the wool to twice the desired width of your strip. Fold the strip in half, and hook with the double thickness.

I Dream in Paisley, 40" x 60", #6- to 8-cut and hand-cut wool, antique challis, and yarn on linen. Designed and hooked by Rae Harrell, Hinesburg, Vermont, 2001.

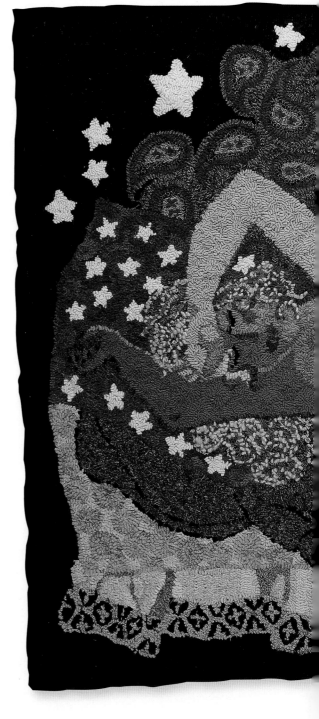

Rae Harrell's self-portraits range from the personally symbolic representation of *Design in Mind* (page 94) to the glamour of *I Dream in Paisley*. With *The Lion Tamer* (page 92), she depicts a time in her life when she, the gorgeous young redhead, "tamed" the handsome bachelor who became her devoted husband, Loy. *My Vote is Peace* (page 94) represents the contemporary Rae, with her silver curls and straightforward opinions. *Time Brings Change and Growth* (page 93) was designed by her daughter when Rae was struggling with the decision to let nature take its course as her red locks turned silver. Each rug tells a story important to Rae about the perception of appearances and their impact on different chapters in her life.

Rae teaches a fascinating method for designing a self-portrait without the use of mirrors or photographs. The resulting hooked rug portraits are remarkable in that the person viewing the portrait can always identify the subject because the designs

capture the essence of their creators, even though they are completed without the assistance of visual aids.

Rae believes our eyes interpret what is seen by our brains. As a result, when we try to translate our mind's image into a sketch, the image is not what we see when we look in the mirror or at a photo. For example, look at your reflection as you start to draw a sketch; you tend to extend the length of the chin by about 25% from reality. Our eyes get the proportions

wrong. Rae's concept in teaching self-portraits is to use one of your senses that she believes is more truthful than vision: the sense of touch. According to Rae, "We have preconceived ideas of what we look like, so we don't believe the vision that comes through our eyes. We believe in our own interpretation. This is why 10 people can draw the same thing and their images will all look different."

Begin by taking a few minutes to explore the contours of your face and head. Feel where your ears are

Self-Portrait, 17" x 21", #6- and 8-cut hand-dyed wool on monk's cloth. Designed and hooked by Priscilla Heininger, Shelburne, Vermont, 2005.

For her background, Priscilla used a single piece of wool. As she cut her strips, she safety-pinned a number to each strip so she could keep track of them and hook them in the order they were cut from the wool.

Shown here are four examples of Rae Harrell's method for designing a self-portrait, which involves the use of no visual aids such as mirrors or photos.

When it comes to measuring the dimensions of your face, Rae Harrell believes your sense of touch is more accurate than your sense of vision. Hands and touch give a truer sense of the features' positions, but your hand tends to be in the same proportion as your face. Use the following steps to measure your face and transfer the proportions to your backing.

1. Lay a piece of backing flat on a table. Stretch out your palm flat on the backing.

2. Note where the center of your hand falls on the backing. Mark this spot; it is where the tip of your nose will fall in the portrait design.

3. The top of your third finger, with your hand still flat on the backing, is where the approximate top of your forehead lies. Mark this spot.

4. The bottom of your palm falls at the bottom of your mouth. Mark this spot.

5. Use your forefinger to note the distance on your face from the bottom of your lip to the bottom of your chin. Lay that finger length on the backing, and mark this spot.

6. Measure one half-finger's length from the hairline up. Mark this spot. It will mark the top of your head on the backing. (The top of your head actually measures longer than this; but you are creating a two-dimensional image, and this one half-finger-length will create good perspective, compensating for the curve of the head.)

7. To duplicate the shape of your face, run your fingers from this part of the dome of your head, down the sides and under to your chin. (Do not start at the crown, but from the part where you can imagine a string holding you up. The crown is too far back.)

8. Draw the shape of your head on the backing, connecting the points you have already marked for the top of your head and the bottom of your chin.

9. Rae encourages her students to hook one half of a face in shadow, using strong contrast in color and value between the two sides of the portrait.

Self Portrait, 17" round, #5- to 8-cut hand-dyed and as-is wool on linen. Designed and hooked by Gail Duclose LaPierre, Shelburne, Vermont, 2006.

Self Portrait, 15½" x 20", #6- and 8-cut hand-dyed and as-is wool on linen. Designed and hooked by Diane Burgess, Hinesburg, Vermont, 2006.

Self Portrait, 16½" x 20", #6- and 7-cut hand-dyed, over-dyed, and as-is wool on monk's cloth. Designed and hooked by Sara Burghoff, Underhill, Vermont, 2010.

The Lion Tamer, 21" x 34", #6- to 8-cut hand-dyed wool on linen. Designed and hooked by Rae Harrell, Hinesburg, Vermont, 1998. From the collection of Ben and Anne-Marie Littenberg.

Time Brings Change and Growth, 31" x 39", #6- to 8-cut hand-dyed wool on linen. Designed by Rebecca Harrell. Hooked by Rae Harrell, Hinesburg, Vermont, 2000.

in relation to your eyes and where your nostrils sit in relation to the corners of your mouth. Where are your eyebrows in relation to the crown of your head? Do you have a prominent jaw line? How is your nose connected to bone? How does the septum relate to the tip of your nose, or the top of your lip? Does your nose turn up or down? How far are your lips from the bottom of your nose? Allow your mind to start making a composite of what you are feeling with your fingers.

Once you have followed the steps in the sidebar, you can make adjustments. Use your fingers like calipers to measure and mark the distance between your eyes (which you will place approximately halfway down the shape of the head you have drawn. For children, the eyes will lie a little lower). Rae encourages her students to draw in the eyes larger than they seem to be in measurement.

My Vote is Peace, 21" x 24", #6- to 8-cut hand-dyed wool on monk's cloth. Designed and hooked by Rae Harrell, Hinesburg, Vermont, 2004.

Design in Mind, 23" x 35", #6- to 8-cut hand-dyed wool on linen. Designed and hooked by Rae Harrell, Hinesburg, Vermont, 2002.

Use your fingers to determine how the bridge of the nose comes down between the eyes. The top of the bridge begins above the center of the eyes. Use your finger to measure your nose's length and mark it on the backing. People tend to draw their noses too long, so watch for this common mistake. Feel where the nostril flare begins, and how the nostrils are separated by the septum. If your nose is turned up, your septum comes down longer than the tip. If it turns down, your nose will be higher and the septum may not be visible.

Use your finger to measure the distance between the septum and the top of your lip. How wide is your lip? Rae says, "This is all a measuring game. Once you get all the basics laid out on the backing, determine where to position your ears. Everyone's ears are different."

This technique of using your hand as a unit of measure provides a basic construct of your own face. According to Rae, "After that, you use a lot of memory. You know if your lower lip is thick or thin. You use your mind's eye rather than mirrors."

With basic proportions and lines drawn in, Rae is ready to hook. She starts by hooking in little circles for parts of the features. For instance, the tip of the nose is basically a little round ball, with two tiny little side balls (like a pawn shop sign). The other little circles of the face include the eyes, cheeks, and chin. Rae suggests hooking these directionally.

Rae hooks the eyes, then moves on to the nose, lips, eyebrows, forehead, chin, and cheeks. She starts filling in the outer shape of the face only when she has completed the rounded contours. "I fill in anything that has prominence first. Then I fill in the recessive areas." She encourages her students to not think too much. "Go with your impulse. The challenge is that the face will seem distorted when you first start hooking your features. You have to get the whole face filled in before you can get a sense of how it will end up looking."

An interesting outcome of this method of designing a self-portrait is that the faces never appear to be smiling. Rather, they each have the look of concentration I expect the designing rug hooker had as she examined and measured her own face, creating the image without the use of mirrors or photos.

CHAPTER 7

Portraits of Pets

F is for Frank, the Gentle King of the Upper Barn, 13½" x 18½", #4-cut hand-dyed wool on monk's cloth. Designed and hooked by Patty Yoder, Tinmouth, Vermont, 2000.

Frank's engaging direct gaze at the viewer adds to the sense of realism in this portrait.

Any of us can take a pencil and draw a quick sketch of a creature we would all be able to identify as a person. Our sketch may be wildly inaccurate, and it may be a terrible drawing, but we are all so familiar with the basic human form that any viewer would instantly understand the figure is supposed to be human.

Is the same true for animals? I might be able to draw a quick sketch of a creature resembling a cat, but I am not sure you would be able to tell if it is meant to be a house cat or something larger and wilder, like a panther. I could also draw

RIGHT: *Ernie, Son of Jack and Jill,* 13¹/₂" x 18¹/₂", #4-cut hand-dyed wool on monk's cloth. Designed and hooked by Patty Yoder, Tinmouth, Vermont, 2000.

Patty allows one of Ernie's woolly locks to dangle in front of his eye, adding a sense of personality and realism. Note how the locks of his fur on his neck and chest are darker than those on the top of his head and shoulders.

LEFT: *Bonnie, Ernie's Sister, the Least Worried of All the Goats in the Upper Barn,* 13¹/₂" x 18¹/₂", #4-cut hand-dyed wool on monk's cloth. Designed and hooked by Patty Yoder, Tinmouth, Vermont, 2000.

Note how Bonnie's head is angled to her left, and the shadow of her muzzle and ruff is visible on her flank.

something resembling a dog, but I am not sure I could draw anything that could be identifiable as a specific breed. I once tried to draw a cow freehand, and it looked more like a moose.

Why is this relevant? My point is it may be much easier to spontaneously create an interesting human portrait from one's imagination. A portrait of a pet may be more challenging to design and execute.

Whether hooking the portrait of a beloved pet, or of some other admired wild animal, begin by spending a lot of time examining photographs. Grab your camera and take pictures of your subject in all positions, engaged in all activities (napping, snacking, chasing a ball). Also,

spend a lot of time on the Internet looking at photos of your particular breed of pet. Be sure to study your own photographs on the computer. The advantage of using the computer screen is that you can zoom in, greatly enlarging the view of small details, thereby enabling you to see things you might not be able to discern with the naked eye and a printed snapshot.

What are the most important details that you wish to get right (ears, muzzle, fur spots and stripes, paw, tail, eyes, head shape, whiskers)? Make a list of these details and then do a specific search for corresponding photos. (I was amazed at the variety of photos I found when using a computer search engine to look for photos of cats' eyes.)

RIGHT: *This Is Jill, Jack's Wife,* 13¹/₂" x 18¹/₂", #4-cut hand-dyed wool on monk's cloth. Designed and hooked by Patty Yoder, Tinmouth, Vermont, 2000.

LEFT: *Save the Elephants,* 26" x 38", #3- to 6-cut hand-dyed wool on linen. Designed and hooked by Donna Hrkman, Dayton, Ohio, 2010. PHOTO COURTESY OF DONNA HRKMAN

Donna did not want to precisely match the natural colors of elephants. "I started pulling out more blues and greens in the gray family and they seemed to combine really well without becoming cartoonish. I am all about shading, so the subtle color gradations were a fun challenge. The lines I use are contoured to show shapes and folds and wrinkles, and even in large flat areas, like the mother elephant's ears, there is direction and movement in the lines."

Study them up close by using your computer to zoom in on the picture, and note what characteristics stand out to you. How do these features differ among breeds or between species? What do the ears of a German shepherd look like when compared to a poodle? What does a dog's pupil look like versus a cat's? Go over the tiniest details of your pictures and decide which characteristics you want to include in your portrait.

When it is time to start drawing your portrait, surround yourself with as many photos as you can. Make some practice sketches. Decide if you are ready to freehand draw your design on your backing, or if you would prefer to use some other design transfer processes explained earlier in this book. You may find you are more dependent on visual references when you design and hook a portrait of a pet than you would be for a human—and this dependence may be the biggest difference between hooking a pet and a human.

Here are some points to keep in mind as you think about animal features.

Hair. We humans style and color our hair in so many different ways; animals don't (although a dog owner may have her pet groomed and clipped, etc.). You have great freedom in designing and hooking hair in a human por-

LEFT: *This Is Earl, Who Was Our First Ram,* 13¹/₂" x 18¹/₂", #4-cut hand-dyed wool on monk's cloth. Designed and hooked by Patty Yoder, Tinmouth, Vermont, 2000.

RIGHT: *Windsong, Who Guards the Animals in the Upper Barn,* 14" x 18¹/₂", #4-cut hand-dyed wool on monk's cloth. Designed and hooked by Patty Yoder, Tinmouth, Vermont, 2000.

Llamas are used to guard sheep from predators such as coyotes. Windsong's intense gaze is perfectly captured here. When you enter the pasture where he stands guard, his head pivots in your direction and he keeps you in his gaze until he feels confident all sheep under his care are safe.

trait. But if you want your animal to be identifiable by breed and species, you must carefully adhere to the appropriate coloring and fur growth patterns, direction, and length.

When hooking human hair, you can take great liberties in your color selection, paying more attention to value. Hooking hair is much trickier with some animals where the color and patterning of fur is specific to a breed or species. For example, in a human you could use dozens of different colored strands of wool to create hair. But could one use as many different colors when hooking a

leopard's spots and still have the subject remain identifiable as a leopard?

When hooking fur that is long, start with the longest strands. Use multiple values that are clearly distinct so you can distinguish individual fur strands. Fill in the shorter hairs later. Note how fur is of varying lengths, textures, color, and value on different parts of a single animal's body and head.

Ears. Human ears are fairly consistent when contrasted with the various sizes and shapes in dogs. Think of the long, droopy, face-framing ears of a bloodhound and

compare those to the triangular shapes of shepherds', which can lie relatively flat or stand high at attention.

Teeth. Showing an animal's teeth will usually add a fierce appearance.

What are the personality characteristics unique to your pet that you want to include in the portrait? For example, your dog may have classic lines and coloring for the breed, but a uniquely distinct way of tilting her head when begging for a treat. Include elements in the design that provide other information unique to that pet, such as a favorite toy ball or a particular neck collar.

Knowing the personality of your subject, and understanding relevant proportion, value, and physiognomy, are the keys to a good hooked rug portrait of your pet.

Buster, 10" x 11", #6- to 8-cut hand-dyed, over-dyed, and as-is wool on linen. Designed and hooked by Diane Phillips, Fairport, New York, 2009.

Buster's personality is portrayed through the unique "flop" of his ears and his distinctive green collar.

Mattie, 18$\frac{1}{2}$" x 22$\frac{1}{2}$", #4- to 6-cut hand-dyed and as-is wool on linen. Designed and hooked by Jen Lavoie, Huntington, Vermont, 2008.

Jen says, "Think more about the personality and characteristics of the dog who is your subject than you do of the photo you use for your visual reference. Use the photo to help you with shape, line, and texture. But find the pose and expression for your composition by thinking about your dog."

Cougar, 10" x 11", #6- to 8-cut hand-dyed, over-dyed, and as-is wool on linen. Designed and hooked by Diane Phillips, Fairport, New York, 2009.

Come Home Mom, 10" x 11", #6- to 8-cut hand-dyed, over-dyed, and as-is wool on linen. Designed and hooked by Diane Phillips, Fairport, New York, 2009.

Jack, Husband of Jill, 13½" x 18½", #4-cut hand-dyed wool on monk's cloth. Designed and hooked by Patty Yoder, Tinmouth, Vermont, 2000.

Toby, 13¹/₂" x 18¹/₂", #4-cut hand-dyed wool on monk's cloth. Designed and hooked by Patty Yoder, Tinmouth, Vermont, 2000.

Curly the Llama, 26" x 20", #4- and 6-cut hand-dyed wool on linen. Designed and hooked by Donna Hrkman, Dayton, Ohio, 2006. PHOTO COURTESY OF DONNA HRKMAN

Gorilla, 14" x 14", #3- and 4-cut hand-dyed wool on verel. Designed and hooked by Jon Ciemiewicz, Hudson, New Hampshire, 2009. PHOTO COURTESY OF JON CIEMIEWICZ

Jon's inspiration for this design was a scene from the stage and screen show, *Cabaret*. "There is a scene were the Master of Ceremonies dances and sings the song 'Cabaret' to an actor in a gorilla costume. It was meant as a way of making fun of the Nazi regime in pre-World War II Germany. This follows a scene where a German woman and Jewish man must break up because of the Nazi takeover. My youngest son is an actor and has played this role on stage." Jon captures enormous intensity and a fierce gaze, which is emphasized by the dark concentric lines around the eyes and strong horizontal lines in the forehead.

CHAPTER 8

Adding Interest

Leo, 24" x 26½", #6- to 8-cut hand-dyed, over-dyed, and as-is wool on linen. Designed and hooked by Diane Phillips, Fairport, New York, 2006.

How can you add interest to your hooked rug portrait? What design elements help distinguish a piece, enhancing the image, making it unique? A precise copy of a photograph is a mere record of what something looks like. An interpretation, expressing a unique vision and style, is more than a record; it is art.

You can make your designs more artistic by 1) adding interest with the lines you use in positioning your subject, 2) including patterns that help tell a story, 3) using unique textures to enhance features, and 4) carefully composing your color palette.

Lines. What is the posture or alignment of your subject? Are you hooking a face that stares straight on from

Free Dance, 27" x 52", #6- to 8-cut hand-dyed, over-dyed, and as-is wool on linen. Designed and hooked by Diane Phillips, Fairport, New York, 2008.

the center of the backing, or is your subject looking off to the side with a tilted head? Is your subject positioned in a way that tells the viewer something about an activity or feeling? Are there lines in the composition that indicate movement to the viewer? The lines can indicate something actually moving through space, as exemplified by the dancer's skirt and hair in Diane Phillips' *Free Dance* (page 109). Or, they can indicate that something is animate, perhaps about to move, as does the dog's ear in Diane Phillips' *Leo* (page 108). Perhaps the lines help the viewer's eye move across the piece, bringing attention and focus to a primary point in the composition. Silver streaks in the hair help point the viewer's eye to the solemn face in Jon Ciemiewicz's *Medicine Woman*. Hands frame the face and the viewer relates to the informal demeanor in Wanda Kerr's

Good Crop, 15" x 20", #2- to 4-cut hand-dyed wool on linen. Designed and hooked by Michele Wise, Seabeck, Washington, 2007. PHOTO COURTESY OF ERIC SCOUTEN

TOP: *Medicine Woman,* 22" x 22", #3-cut wool and sport-weight yarn on verel. Hooked and designed by Jon Ciemiewicz, Hudson, New Hampshire, 2007, as inspired by a painting by Frank Howell. PHOTO COURTESY OF JON CIEMIEWICZ

ABOVE: *The Goddess Reflects,* 21" x 12", #3- to 5-cut hand-dyed wool and nylon hose on linen. Designed and hooked by Wanda Kerr, Wiarton, Ontario, Canada, 2008. PHOTO COURTESY OF WANDA KERR

The Power of Red Shoes, 27" x 48", #6- and 8-cut hand-dyed and as-is wool with various embellishments (buttons, old earrings, antique Irish lace, etc.) on linen. Designed and hooked by Suzanne Dirmaier, Waterbury Center, Vermont, 2003.

LEFT: *Ginkgos and Grammys,* 21" x 29", #8-cut hand-dyed wool on linen. Designed and hooked by Sharon Townsend, Altoona, Iowa, and Marathon, Florida, 2005. PHOTO COURTESY OF TOM TUSSEY

ABOVE: *Strong Woman,* 14³/₄" x 24¹/₂", #6- and 8-cut hand-dyed wool on monk's cloth. Designed and hooked by Priscilla Heininger, Shelburne, Vermont, 2009.

The Goddess Reflects (page 111). The lines of rippling wheat in Michele Wise's *Good Crop* (page 110) leave the impression that a gentle breeze is blowing as two women walk the field. The kick of a red-shod foot lets the viewer know the subject has spunk, personality, and a sense of style in Suzanne Dirmaier's *The Power of Red Shoes* (page 111).

Pattern. A pattern or repeated motif can provide information suggesting a story line, as exemplified in the details of *Looking for Red Shoes* (page 42). A pattern of swirling blue in the background of

Susan, 21" x 23", hand-cut, hand-dyed wool on rug warp. Designed and hooked by Jule Marie Smith, Ballston Spa, New York, 2006.

Priscilla Heininger's *Strong Woman* helps set the mood by suggesting the subject is vibrant and alive. The sense of mood would be very different in this portrait if the background were hooked with a single, flat color in straight rows. In *Gingkos and Grammys* (page 112), a circular pattern frames each face, helping to keep each portrait from getting lost in the rest of the composition. A row of stars emphasizes the patriotic subject portrayed in *Susan B.*

Anthony by Diane Phillips. In addition, they add a touch of whimsy to an otherwise stern portrait. A background of multihued squares adds precision to the fantasy face in Jule Marie Smith's *Susan.*

Texture. Texture can add interest and emphasis. It draws the viewer closer to the piece. Texture can be achieved by using an unusual rug hooking "stitch." For example, the background for Peg Irish's *A Head Above the*

Susan B. Anthony, 15" x 26", #6- to 8-cut hand-dyed, over-dyed, and as-is wool on linen. Designed and hooked by Diane Phillips, Fairport, New York, 2006.

Looking for Red Shoes (detail) by Suzanne Dirmaier. (See the full rug on page 42.)

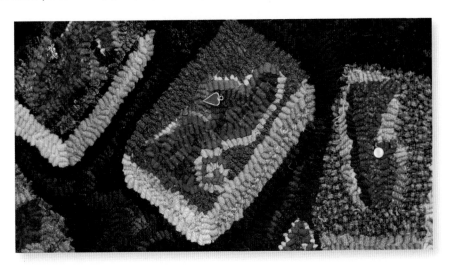

A Head Above the Rest, 24" x 30", #3-cut hand-dyed wool on cotton foundation. Designed and hooked by Peg Irish, Madbury, New Hampshire, 1999.

The frame is enhanced by computer-generated images printed on cotton.

Captain Fantastic, 51" x 45", hand- and commercially dyed and spun, one- and two-ply, bulky and fine, straight spun and bouclé yarns (wool, mohair, silk, and angora), and roving on linen. Designed and hooked by Heidi Wulfraat, Lakeburn, New Brunswick, Canada, 2008. PHOTO COURTESY OF HEIDI WULFRAAT

A Face in the Crowd was inspired by the crowds of people I saw at a concert of a popular rock and roll band. I took dozens of photos of the people around me. One image was particularly memorable: a young man with a flat face and wildly tousled hair. The crowd was surging, the music was pulsing, and he had a blank, startled look on his face, as if he had been awakened from a nap. This rug looks nothing like him, but it embodies my memory of the subject. It is the first portrait I hooked. If this rug was hooked by someone else and I was critiquing it, these are the points I would offer for consideration:

A Face in the Crowd, 18¼" x 18¼", #8-cut hand-dyed wool on monk's cloth. Designed and hooked by Anne-Marie Littenberg, Burlington, Vermont, 2004.

- I like the use of light, medium, dark, and very dark values in the hair. I like the wild lines, and the use of directional hooking, which helps to delineate individual strands.
- I like that the subject is gazing just a bit off to the side. The viewer does not know what the subject is looking at.
- I like the ambiguous expression of the subject. I can read many possibilities here: grim, thoughtful, startled.
- I cannot tell if this figure is a man or a woman. The broad shoulders and strong neck suggest a man . . . the shape of the eyes and intense color of the lips suggest a woman wearing makeup. (An earring and patterned shirt are not dependable cues for figuring this out.)
- The boldly patterned shirt is a bit of a distraction. Because it is bright red, the viewer's eye goes to it first, before moving up to the face. This gives the shirt more impact than I intended; the rug is supposed to be about the face. Making this image even more of a close-up, eliminating most of the shoulders and background, would put stronger focus on the face.
- The swirly background, patterned shirt, wild hair, and strongly pigmented wool hooked into the face suggest a lot of movement in this rug. The eye has no place to rest. A simpler background would have been more effective. The swirls would work better if the background were a single piece of flat or gently mottled wool in a single color.
- More subtle transition between the values used for the lines and skin of the face would have resulted in a gentler appearance.
- There are too many different, unrelated colors here. I would prefer to see less variety in color. Or, keep a great variety of color in the palette for the face and hair, but then simplify color in the shirt and background.

Rest (page 116) is hooked in reverse; you see the backs of the loops on the front of the rug. The resulting texture serves to emphasize the details of the #3-cut hooked loops (which are right side up) used in the face.

Texture can also be achieved by hooking with fibers that have unique qualities (such as wool roving instead of wool strips) and using loops of differing cuts and heights. Heidi Wulfraat traditionally hooks with a variety of hand- and commercially dyed and spun yarns in a num-

ber of different plies: fibers ranging from wool, mohair, and silk to angora and roving. When you see *Captain Fantastic* in real life, you are drawn to the ways the different looped materials reflect light. The loops formed through hooking look as unique and interesting as the different fibers used in the yarns. Together they provide much greater textural variety than if the artist had solely used cut wool strips.

Self Portrait, 15" x 15", #3- to 6-cut hand-dyed wool and yarn on monk's cloth. Designed and hooked by Barbara Held, Tinmouth, Vermont, 2005.

Wanda Kerr used a variety of sizes in her cut wool strips in *The Goddess Reflects* (page 111). In addition, she used dyed nylons. According to Wanda, when you use wide strips, you have to edit because they "speak strong." With narrow cuts, you can throw in many strips and have more room to go awry because smaller loops hide more easily among the rest. With wide strips, every single loop is easily visible. Jon Ciemiewicz once told me that he finds hooking with a #3 cut easier than a wide cut, because you don't have to be so worried about the precision of your loops.

Barbara Held's *Self Portrait* added a lot of interesting texture by using novelty wool yarns to portray her curly silver hair. Barb hooked the face using a subtle value mix of cut wool. The transition between strips of wool in her skin is subtle, because rather than hook loops that are neatly aligned, she skewered each loop so they go every which way. This crazy mix results in a texture that softly blends the lines between contiguous strips of wool in different colors and values. The skin has a soft, unlined, luminous quality. If all her loops were perfectly straight and aligned, the lines in her face would have been distinct and perhaps severe.

Wanda Kerr's *Woolvis Proddly* uses the proddy technique for this portrait of "The King of Rock and Roll." The prodded pieces give the piece an effect reminiscent of

impasto in painting, where pigment is heavily spread, sometimes with a blade rather than brush. Suzanne Dirmaier mixed proddy and traditional hooking in *The Spirit of My Hollow Tree*.

Color. As you glance through the hooked rug portraits featured in this book, colors range from realistic to fantastic. Some rug hookers use only the most realistic colors, hues, and tones. Others explore the possibilities of extravagant coloration, depending on value and proportion to help the viewer understand what he or she is seeing. Some color plan their rugs and carefully custom dye their swatches. Others use as-is scraps that are readily at hand. Either option works beautifully. You must decide what works best for you.

Your use of line and color have enormous impact on the way the hooked rug portrait is perceived. For example, compare Diane Kelly's *Once Strong, Now Alzheimers*, with Laura Pierce's *Laura at Cambria* (both on page 120). Color and line in the subjects' faces tell the viewer two completely different stories about these women. You want to sit down with Laura for some fine conversation and perhaps some rug hooking. *Once Strong* shocks the viewer, forcing him or her to think of something disturbing. Diane Phillips' *Sam* (page 121) is hooked with fairly

Woolvis Proddly, 13" x 18³/₄", wide prodded strips of wool on linen. Designed and prodded by Wanda Kerr, Wiarton, Ontario, Canada, 1998. PHOTO COURTESY OF WANDA KERR

The Spirit of My Hollow Tree, 31" x 26", #8- and 4-cut hand-dyed wool, roving, and ribbon on linen. Designed, hooked, and prodded by Suzanne Dirmaier, Waterbury Center, Vermont, 2003.

LEFT: *Once Strong, Now Alzheimer's,* 19½" x 20½", #6- to 8-cut hand-dyed wool on linen. Designed and hooked by Diane Kelly, Dorset, Vermont, 2005.

BELOW: *Laura at Cambria,* 10" x 14", #8-cut hand-dyed and as-is wool on linen. Designed and hooked by Laura Pierce, Petaluma, California, 2008. PHOTO COURTESY OF LAURA PIERCE

conventional colors, but the happy explosion of colorful shapes in the background adds a strong sense of fun and whimsy.

Diane Phillips hooks both realistically and fantastically colored portraits. She is especially fond of working with whatever scraps of wool are within easy reach. However, for a new rug hooker, it can be difficult to get the hang of putting highly unusual colors (like green or purple) into a face. Sometimes our brains are entrenched in trying to perfectly mimic reality. If you would like to explore hooking a face with unusual colors, Diane suggests an exercise to get you going. Think of a portrait painted by a 19th century impressionistic painter such as Vincent van Gogh. Try to hook a small mat precisely copying every line and color you find in that original painting. Make your rendition as perfect and precise as you can, mimicking lines of paint with directional hooking. This exercise will teach you a great deal about how dabs and lines in red, green, purple, and orange can be used for shadows and features. In fact, you may not even realize those colors are present in the portrait until you have actually explored every inch of the image.

If you are creating your own design, Diane suggests using three different kinds of colored wool for your

Sam, 15½" x 15½", #7-cut hand-dyed, over-dyed, and as-is wool on linen. Designed and hooked by Diane Phillips, Fairport, New York, 1998.

skin tones: one third of it should be of a light value in a fairly realistic color; one third should be in a dark value of a fairly realistic color; and one third can be made up of a variety of wild colors and values.

Diane has a great trick for coming up with that one-third batch of wild colors. Collect about 10 to 12 small pieces of wool. They can be strips that are 2" by 8". There should be a lot of different values in the mix (light, medium, and dark). Be careful you don't use a lot of red because it will give the entire batch a pink cast. Pile the strips in a neat, flat bundle, one on top of the other. Place them in an empty dye pot. Gently fill the pot with enough tepid water so the wool is just covered, but not full enough for the pieces to move around. Note: You are

not presoaking this wool, nor are you using a wetting agent (synthrapol) or salt. Put the pot on the stove, turn on the heat, and add a splash of ammonia to the water. Watch the pot. While the wool is cooking, you want the pieces to touch each other, but you do not want them to move around the pot. As soon as you see the colors start to bleed, pour in the acid, turn off the heat, and let the strips cool down while sitting in the dye bath. Do not stir. When the dye pot and wool are cooled to room temperature, wash the wool in your washing machine on the gentle cycle with cold water and a drop of detergent for two minutes. Allow it to go through the entire rinse cycle. Throw the wool in the clothes dryer with a fabric-softening sheet and a bath towel. This dye technique is a great

Othello, 23" x 23", #6- to 8-cut hand-dyed wool on monk's cloth. Designed and hooked by Gloria Reynolds Stokes, Hinesburg, Vermont, 2005.

Vermont Vignette: Earthquake, 14" x 12", #3- and 6-cut hand-dyed wool on cotton foundation, embellished with printed cotton rug. Designed and hooked by Peg Irish, Madbury, New Hampshire, 2003.

Peg and her husband Jim were surprised during one visit to Vermont by an earthquake that shook them up in their motel room. Peg says, "What could be better than to hook the two of us being shaken out of our bed? I put on my nightgown and asked Jim to photograph me almost falling out of bed. Then I asked him to get in bed and look up with the 'what is she up to now' look and it only took one photo to capture that pose. I added a picture of a covered bridge on the wall, which was very crooked. Then I took a photo of one of my rugs, distorted it with Photoshop software, printed it out on cotton, and appliquéd it to the hooked piece."

Steve Fish (shirt detail) by Patty Yoder. The perfectly hooked plaid pattern, showing natural lines and folds, adds a sense of realism. (See the full rug on page 53.)

way to take a variety of unrelated scraps and make them work together. The pieces pick up spots of colors from each other. Balance this dramatic batch of "married" wools with some of the more realistic dye formulas in the Dye Formulas for Skin Tones sidebar (page 130).

Llarry the Llama, 27" x 31", #4- and 6-cut hand-dyed wool strips and alpaca fleece yarn on linen. Designed and hooked by Donna Hrkman, Dayton, Ohio, 2006. PHOTO COURTESY OF DONNA HRKMAN

According to Donna, "I wanted to explore the cultural inspiration of where llamas come from, so I did some research on the Incan culture. The vivid rust colors are found in many Incan fabric goods. The zigzag pattern at the top of the rug is taken from Incan woven belt designs, and the striped panels on the sides are taken from Incan rug weavings. Llarry's long locks are actually strands of natural alpaca yarn, spun from fleece."

Emmy, 16" x 16", #3- to 6-cut as-is and hand-dyed wool on linen. Designed and hooked by Laura Pierce. PHOTO COURTESY OF LAURA PIERCE

The design was inspired by a photograph Laura took of her daughter 25 years ago.

Amelia, 15 1/2" x 15 1/2", hand-cut, hand-dyed wool on rug warp. Designed and hooked by Jule Marie Smith, Ballston Spa, New York, 2005.

Note the textile patternings on Amelia's blouse and headscarf and how their colors are repeated in the sky.

Hang Five, 20" x 24", #3- to 8-cut over-dyed and as-is wool on linen burlap.
Designed and hooked by Diane Learmonth, Anacortes, Washington, 2008. PHOTO
COURTESY OF C. DENNIS MAYER

Pattern and plaid stripes contrast with the organic shapes of the portrait subject.

Going to Pieces, 25" x 40",
#8-cut hand-dyed wool on
linen. Designed and hooked by
Sharon Townsend, Altoona, Iowa,
and Marathon, Florida, 2004.
PHOTO COURTESY OF TOM TUSSEY

This self-portrait takes the shape
of a puzzle pattern. Sharon says,
"I drew the picture and then divided
each section into a puzzle piece, giving
each section its own motif: circles on
the eye pieces, checks on the cheeks,
and paisley on the mouth. The neck and
top of the head had stripes and the nose
was plain. I bound each piece separately
and then basted them together and steamed
the whole piece. Eventually I took out the
basting, and the grandchildren play with the
big puzzle rug.

Witchy Woman, 13" x 13", #6-cut hand-dyed wool on linen. Designed and hooked by Diane Phillips, Fairport, New York, 2006.

The lines and motion of fire are repeated in Witchy Woman's hair.

Magda, 14³/₄" x 15", hand-cut, hand-dyed wool on rug warp. Designed and hooked by Jule Marie Smith, Ballston Spa, New York, 2004.

Desdemona, 22" x 27", #6-cut hand-dyed wool and beaded embellishment on monk's cloth. Designed and hooked by Barbara Held, Tinmouth, Vermont, 2006.

These formulas were created by Diane Phillips. The dyes are all Pro-Chem Washfast Acid Dyes.

Use half of the following formulas to dye $^1/_2$ yard of natural or white wool. Use the second half of the formula batch to dye an additional $^1/_8$ of a yard. These two sessions will provide you with wool for light skin tones and corresponding wool for shadows.

Light Skin Tones. Use for $^1/_2$ yard of white or natural wool.

- *Geisha:* $^1/_{128}$ t. #502 chocolate brown; $^1/_{128}$ t. #560 chestnut; $^1/_{128}$ t. #130 caramel; one toothpick #440 blue.

- *Elizabeth I:* $^1/_{128}$ t. #130 caramel; $^1/_{64}$ t. #135 yellow; $^1/_{128}$ t. #349 fuchsia; $^1/_{128}$ t. #725 green; $^1/_{128}$ t. #560 chestnut.

- *Nordic Beauty:* $^1/_{128}$ t. #502 chocolate brown; $^1/_{64}$ t. #560 chestnut; $^1/_{128}$ t. #130 caramel; toothpick #440 blue.

Medium Skin Tones. Use for $^1/_2$ yard of white or natural wool.

- *Mary Magdalene:* $^1/_{128}$ t. #502 chocolate brown; $^1/_{128}$ t. #560 chestnut; $^1/_{128}$ t. #130 caramel.

- *La Azteca:* $^1/_{16}$ t. #130 caramel; $^1/_{32}$ t. #560 chestnut; $^1/_{128}$ t. #255 brick.

- *Nomad:* $^1/_{16}$ t. #130 caramel; $^1/_8$ t. #233 orange; $^1/_{64}$ t. #413 navy; $^1/_{64}$ t. #822 plum.

Dark Skin Tones. Use for $^1/_2$ yard of white or natural wool.

- *Indira:* $^1/_{16}$ t. #502 chocolate brown; $^1/_{16}$ t. #560 chestnut; $^1/_{16}$ t. + $^1/_{32}$ t. #130 caramel.

- *Aretha:* $^1/_{64}$ t. #822 plum; $^1/_{64}$ t. #255 brick; $^1/_{128}$ t. #560 chestnut; $^1/_4$ t. + $^1/_{16}$ t. #502 chocolate brown.

- *Nefertiti:* $^1/_{16}$ t. #255 brick; $^1/_{16}$ t. #502 chocolate brown; $^1/_{16}$ t. #560 chestnut; $^1/_{16}$ t. #672 black; $^1/_{16}$ t. #822 plum.

CHAPTER 9

Expressing Your Unique Point of View

So many factors go into making a hooked rug portrait unique. As you explore many options for style, color, and subject, I encourage you to express your own unique point of view.

Some hooked rug portraits are perfect copies of photographs. Others are portraits that show a wide range of facial expressions. Some capture a moment in time or memory. A few have a message, telling a powerful story. These portraits are more than just a record; they evoke a strong emotional response.

Evoking an emotional response is what I believe elevates craft to art. It doesn't matter if the response is positive or negative, happy or sad. Rather, the importance lies in the intensity of the response and whether it causes the viewer to pause and think, even if only for a brief moment. Such a response might be, "I miss my dog" or "That makes me uncomfortable" or "I wish I knew that person" or "I remember when..." or "How did she do that?" or "That makes me happy."

I first saw Heidi Wulfraat's *Love on the Run* a number of years ago at one of the Green Mountain Rug Hooking Guild's exhibits at Shelburne Museum in Shelburne, Vermont. That year, the show had over 700 rugs on exhibit, and it was overwhelming. The rugs rose from the floors to the rafters, covering every conceivable inch of space. Heidi's rug ended up very high on a wall, and even though the volume of rugs was so huge I can hardly remember what else was on exhibit, *Love on the Run* stayed with me. It is one of my all-time favorite hooked rugs. I loved how the subject, a dog named

Love on the Run, 27" x 53", hand- and commercially dyed wool yarns and roving on Scottish burlap. Designed and hooked by Heidi Wulfraat, Lakeburn, New Brunswick, Canada, 2005. PHOTO COURTESY OF HEIDI WULFRAAT

Farmer, is positioned on the lower left of the rug. His posture, erect ears, and tail let me know he is very interested in something off in the distance. And he is not alone. You see the legs of his mistress in the distance, positioned in the upper right of the rug. Heidi's use of color, design and perspective are terrific, and her subject brought me to a fond memory of my own walks with beloved dogs.

The Cocoon and the Bed Skirt depicts a quiet, intimate moment that any of us might relate to. Is the subject waking from a nap, recovering from illness, deep in thought, or engaged in conversation with someone out of view? Rachelle LeBlanc hooked a series called "Fleeting Moments," which she says, "explores the passing moments that remind us of something precious, some-

Summer Days Dream, 19^1/$_2$" x 39^1/$_2$", hand-cut and hand-dyed wool and cashmere on linen. Designed and hooked by Rachelle LeBlanc, St. Albert, Alberta, Canada, 2009. PHOTO COURTESY OF RACHELLE LEBLANC

The Cocoon and the Bed Skirt, 48" x 34", hand-cut and dyed cashmere on linen. Designed and hooked by Rachelle LeBlanc, St. Albert, Alberta, Canada, 2010. PHOTO COURTESY OF RACHELLE LEBLANC

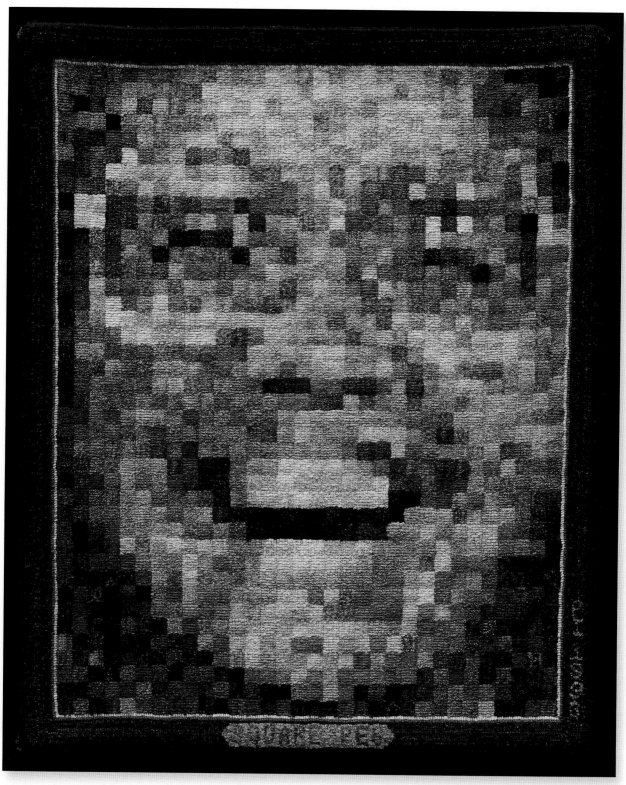

Square Peg, 20" x 24",
#3-cut hand-dyed wool on
cotton foundation. Designed
and hooked by Peg Irish,
Madbury, Vermont, 1993.

thing that is hard to identify and thought forgotten. The importance of these moments reminds us that we should all take time to see the beauty that surrounds us." *Summer Days Dream* (page 133) is another sweet, intimate moment, perhaps between a mother and daughter.

Peg Irish has always been on the forefront of exploring new ideas and techniques in rug hooking. One might think *Square Peg* was inspired by today's ubiquitous use of digital photography and computer-generated images. However, this rug was begun in 1990,

My Ropes, 38" x 28", #4- to 7-cut, new and recycled hand-dyed wool and other fabric strips plus rope embellishment on linen.
Designed and hooked by Linda Rae Coughlin, Warren, New Jersey, 1999.   PHOTO COURTESY OF LINDA RAE COUGHLIN

way before most of us had ever even heard of a pixel, including Peg. This piece was inspired by quilting. Peg had her husband, Jim, photograph her, and then she used a photocopier to enlarge the image to 8" by 10". Peg took a piece of clear plastic, drew a grid of $^1/_2$" squares, and placed it over the enlarged image. As she hooked, she carefully studied each little square. Thus, in 1990, Peg managed to create a piece like no other hooked rug portrait, and something that looks more like it comes from 2010. She achieved this incredibly modern design using a centuries-old copying technique: the grid method discussed in earlier chapters. Peg says, "I don't draw. I rely almost entirely on photography. I generally work with the photos at my computer [although with *Square Peg* she used the photocopier since 1990 was before the time when we all used digital photography]. Eventually I tend to use the transfer pencil to get the important lines on my backing. With *Square Peg*, I just created a grid of squares and highlighted a few elements: the mouth, eyeglasses, etc."

Linda Rae Coughlin's hooked rug art is about being fearless and having a vision that demands to be expressed. Her hooked rugs are not about decorating. She is not concerned with rules about what colors may or may not be used together. She says, "I never know what will come up next, but when it does, I run with it."

Linda's rugs are always autobiographical. *My Ropes* is her funeral rug. *No, Watch Your Back* (page 137) is about being over-burdened. *No Brave Soul* (page 136) was actually hooked before she had a personal health scare. Linda sketches and photographs, using any method possible to capture an image. The final pieces may not physically resemble her, but she still uses herself as the model. Words are often an important part of her designs. Sometimes the words inspire the images, and sometimes an image enters her head and the corresponding words come later. Inspiration comes from a wide range of sources. For example, an image she saw in the pattern of a marble wall inspired her funeral piece, like a Rorschach test. She sees faces and patterns in unexpected places.

No Brave Soul, 20" x 23", #4- to 7-cut hand-dyed new and recycled wool and other fabric strips plus machine embroidery and fleece on linen. Designed and hooked by Linda Rae Coughlin, Warren, New Jersey, 2000. PHOTO COURTESY OF LINDA RAE COUGHLIN

Linda spends a great deal of time thinking about a new idea. She always keeps a little sketch pad at hand for quick drawings and notes. Linda says she decides on her color palette before she begins hooking. She may change her designs, but she always sticks with her original idea for the color palette. She thinks too often rug hookers use too many colors. She believes in limiting the palette, generally sticking to about four different colors, and focusing more on value. She uses a lot of recycled material and other elements, and she likes trying other fibers like stockings and synthetics, but she prefers wool because of the color control she achieves in her dyeing.

No, Watch Your Back, 30" x 33", #4- to 7-cut hand-dyed new and recycled wool and other fabrics plus machine embroidery, fleece, ribbon, and burlap tape on linen. Designed and hooked by Linda Rae Coughlin, Warren, New Jersey, 2009. PHOTO COURTESY OF LINDA RAE COUGHLIN

Linda is not concerned with whether the viewer is able to read the words she hooks. Sometimes her work involves redoing. If something bothers her, she pulls it out right away and does it over until she gets it right. But when she is done with a rug, it is done. She never rehooks once it is completed. Linda says, "Rules are meant to be broken. Find your own path and don't be dragged down by rules."

I have been fascinated by personal qualities that make someone identifiable, even if you don't see their face. You can be in a room with friends and family and know who they are even when their backs are to you. *How Do I Get From Here to the Rest of the World* (page 138) is a portrait of my husband, Ben. He is easily identified by those

who know him from the angle of his shoulder, the rolled shirt sleeve, and old, worn blue jeans.

I photographed Ben close up, from behind. I wanted the finished rug to be larger than life. I printed an 8" by 10" copy of the photo and took it to my local copy center, where they enlarged it to larger than life. I transferred his image to the backing, copying exactly the shadows, folds, and seams of his clothes. The shirt he wore for the photo was blue, but I wanted something warmer. The landscape that constitutes the rest of the composition comes from

my imagination. Although I drew his figure precisely, the rest of the backing just had a few lines to indicate the receding road and distant mountains. The details of the landscape I hooked spontaneously. I did have to rehook the road multiple times to achieve the effect I wanted. When I plan a rug, I have no idea what it will look like when finished. But as soon as I do something I find displeasing, I tear it out and rework it.

I like this piece because it is so ambiguous. Is he looking at the distance with hope, sorrow, expectation, or

fear? Although the rug is intensely personal to me, each viewer has his or her own individual response to it.

Look through old family photographs. Sit in a café and do some people-watching. Visit an art museum. Cruise the Internet. Find inspiration for your own hooked rug portrait. Give thought to the tips, tricks, and ideas provided here, but venture out on your own and explore what pleases you.

How Do I Get From Here to the Rest of the World?, 74" x 38", plied threads on cotton rug warp. Designed and hooked by Anne-Marie Littenberg, Burlington, Vermont, 2009.

RESOURCES

Bee-Line Townsend
Fabric Cutting Tools
rughooker@beeline-co.com
866-218-1590
www.beeline-townsend.com

Bolivar Cutters
Joan@swimmingcat.com
PO Box 539
Bridgewater, Nova Scotia
Canada
B4V 2X6
902-543-7762
www.bolivarcutter.com

The Dorr Mill Store
22 Hale Street, PO Box 88
Guild, NH 03754
1-800-846-3677
www.dorrmillstore.com

Susan Feller
Ruckman Mill Farm
PO Box 409
Augusta, WV 26704
304-496-8073
info@RuckmanMillFarm.com
www.ruckmanmillfarm.com

Green Mountain Hooked Rugs
2838 Country Road
Montpelier, Vermont 05602
802-223-1333
www.greenmountainhookedrugs.com

Jim Lilly
304-496-8073
www.artwools.com

Rae Harrell Studio
90 Mechanicsville Road
Hinesburg, VT 05461
802-734-7363
raeharrell@gmavt.net

Amy Oxford
The Oxford Company
445 Swamp Road
Cornwall VT 05753
802-462-2011
www.amyoxford.com

Diane Phillips
Dye Formulas for Hooked Faces
10 Periwinkle Drive
Fairport, NY 14450
585-223-0038

Pro-Chem Washfast Acid Dyes
1-800-228-9393